ASSESSING THE POTENTIAL OF TRADE ALONG THE PROPOSED SHYMKENT–TASHKENT–KHUJAND ECONOMIC CORRIDOR

JANUARY 2021

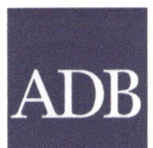

© 2021 Asian Development Bank
6 ADB Avenue, Mandaluyong City, 1550 Metro Manila, Philippines
Tel +63 2 8632 4444; Fax +63 2 8636 2444
www.adb.org

Some rights reserved. Published in 2021.

ISBN 978-92-9262-625-9 (print); 978-92-9262-626-6 (electronic); 978-92-9262-627-3 (ebook)
Publication Stock No. TCS200413-2
DOI: http://dx.doi.org/10.22617/TCS200413-2

The views expressed in this publication are those of the authors and do not necessarily reflect the views and policies of the Asian Development Bank (ADB) or its Board of Governors or the governments they represent.

ADB does not guarantee the accuracy of the data included in this publication and accepts no responsibility for any consequence of their use. The mention of specific companies or products of manufacturers does not imply that they are endorsed or recommended by ADB in preference to others of a similar nature that are not mentioned.

By making any designation of or reference to a particular territory or geographic area, or by using the term "country" in this document, ADB does not intend to make any judgments as to the legal or other status of any territory or area.

Please contact pubsmarketing@adb.org if you have questions or comments with respect to content, or if you wish to obtain copyright permission for your intended use that does not fall within these terms, or for permission to use the ADB logo.

Corrigenda to ADB publications may be found at http://www.adb.org/publications/corrigenda.

Note:
In this publication, "$" refers to United States dollar, "SUM" refers to sum, and "T" refers to tenge.

Cover design by Principe Nicdao.

On the cover: Features representing main sectors and areas (transport connectivity, agriculture value chain, sanitary and phytosanitary measures, tourism) for the Shymkent-Tashkent-Khujand Economic Corridor development (photos from the ADB Photo Library).

Contents

Tables and Figures

Abbreviations

ADB	Asian Development Bank
BCP	border crossing point
CAREC	Central Asia Regional Economic Cooperation
CIS	Commonwealth of Independent States
CPMM	Corridor Performance Measurement and Monitoring
CWRC	Regional Cooperation and Operations Coordination Division of the Central and West Asia Department
EAEU	Eurasian Economic Union
EU	European Union
FTA	free trade area
GDP	gross domestic product
MFN	most favored nation
TCI	trade complementarity index
RCAI	revealed comparative advantage index
STKEC	Shymkent–Tashkent–Khujand Economic Corridor
UN	United Nations
US	United States
WB	World Bank
WTO	World Trade Organization

Acknowledgments

This study was undertaken on behalf of the Central Asia Regional Economic Cooperation (CAREC) Secretariat of the Asian Development Bank (ADB) under the ADB technical assistance (TA) 9630: Assessing Economic Corridor Development Potential among Kazakhstan, Uzbekistan, and Tajikistan. Safdar Parvez, director of the Regional Cooperation and Operations Coordination Division of the Central and West Asia Department (CWRC) of ADB provided overall guidance; and Xinglan Hu, principal regional cooperation specialist of CWRC managed the TA project. Irene De Roma, programs officer, and Maria Cecilia Sison, operations assistant, CWRC, supported the TA implementation including organizing the TA inception missions, regional consultation workshops, and the publication of this report. The TA team also included international and national consultants: Roman Mogilevskii (lead author of the report), Aradhna Aggarwal, Bahodir Ganiev, Patricia Georgina Gonzales, Umida Haknazar, Shuhrat Nurubloev, and Sergey Solodovnik. Government agencies, business communities, and development partners in Kazakhstan, Uzbekistan, and Tajikistan provided data and inputs to this report.

Guntur Sugiyarto, principal economist; Oleg Samukhin, senior transport specialist; Dorothea Lazaro, regional cooperation specialist; and Carmen Maria Garcia Perez, regional cooperation specialist of ADB, conducted peer reviews on the draft report.

The TA team expresses its appreciation to Guldana Sadykova, Ganjina Fazilova, and Rovshan Mamurov, CAREC Regional Cooperation Coordinator for Kazakhstan, Tajikistan, and Uzbekistan respectively, for their support in the implementation of the TA, including coordinating with the multi-stakeholders, organizing the inception missions and regional consultation workshops, and facilitating field studies in the three countries. The TA team thanks ADB-based national consultants Jennifer Lapis and Alzeus Alzate for their support in organizing TA-related workshops.

The TA team is grateful to ADB staff at headquarters and at the resident missions in Kazakhstan, Uzbekistan, and Tajikistan for their support and inputs.

The TA and all its activities are funded by the People's Republic of China Poverty Reduction and Regional Cooperation Fund.

1 Introduction

1.   This report was prepared under the technical assistance: Assessing the Economic Corridor Development Potential among Kazakhstan, Uzbekistan, and Tajikistan of the Asian Development Bank (ADB). It aims to determine the trade potential along the proposed Shymkent–Tashkent–Khujand Economic Corridor (STKEC). It specifically measures the trade that is currently transpiring in Shymkent city and Turkestan oblast of Kazakhstan, Sugd oblast of Tajikistan, and Tashkent city and Tashkent oblast of Uzbekistan. The report also covers transit trade along the STKEC and the three countries' trade in services related to STKEC region, and discusses their trade regimes. It then provides an analysis of the existing trade barriers and opportunities for trade expansion, and how these barriers can be addressed in the framework of the STKEC development. The report concludes with recommendations to trade stakeholders in the STKEC region.

2.   All data used in the report were from the official sources of Kazakhstan, Tajikistan, and Uzbekistan; and from ADB and other international organizations, except when sources are explicitly indicated.

2 Current Situation and Trends in Trade

2.1. Kazakhstan

2.1.1. Trade in Goods

3.	The exports of Kazakhstan are very much dependent on international prices, especially for its main export commodity—crude oil (Figures 1). The hike in oil prices during 2011–2013 and the oil prices' fall during 2015–2016 resulted in big fluctuations in the country's total exports. Other key export products of Kazakhstan are ferrous and nonferrous metals, ores and concentrates, and wheat and wheat flour.

4.	As imports in Kazakhstan are mostly financed by export revenue, the dynamics of imports and exports are very similar. The key imports include machinery and equipment, chemicals and plastics, iron and steel and articles thereof, and agrifood products.

5.	The main trade partners of Kazakhstan for exports and for imports are the European Union (EU), the Russian Federation, and the People's Republic of China (PRC). In 2018, the share of these three main partners was 70% in total merchandise exports and 75% in total imports. Other important trade partners include the Republic of Korea, Switzerland, the United States (US), and countries of Central Asia.

6.	The fluctuations in international oil prices impacted the dynamics of merchandise exports and imports—expressed as a percentage of gross domestic product (GDP). Exports as percentage of GDP achieved its highest value at 46% in 2011, falling to just 25% in 2015, then partly recovering to 36% in 2018. Imports were less volatile, remaining in the range of 17%–21% of GDP and accounting for 19% of GDP in 2018.

2.1.2. Trade in Services

7.	The dynamics of trade in services in Kazakhstan mostly replicate the dynamics of merchandise trade (Figures 2). This should be expected as most of the service exports and imports are related to the transport of goods, technical (e.g., geological explorations), and business services for oil production and other commodity export sectors. The growth in the total export of services is mostly due to the pipeline transport serving the transit of Turkmenistan and Uzbekistan natural gas to the PRC and to the Russian Federation. Still, the revenue from the export of services is not very high at 12% in 2018 when compared to the revenue of merchandise export. Imports of services are considered important in Kazakhstan, accounting for 36% of the import of goods in 2018. The exports and imports of tourism services are also large—at $2.0 billion (for exports) and $2.5 billion (for imports) in 2018.

Figure 1: Kazakhstan—Merchandise Trade

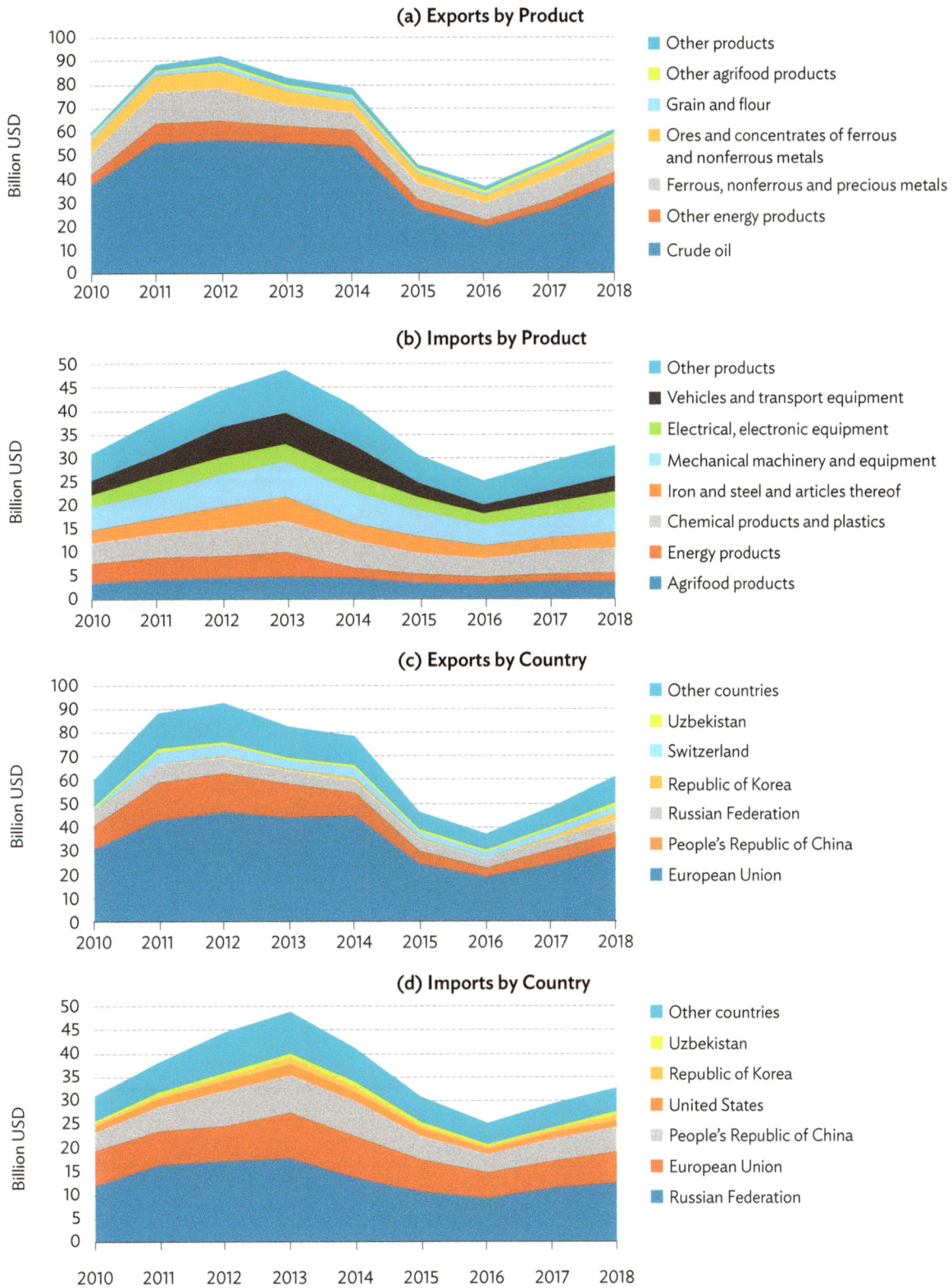

(a) Exports by Product

Legend:
- Other products
- Other agrifood products
- Grain and flour
- Ores and concentrates of ferrous and nonferrous metals
- Ferrous, nonferrous and precious metals
- Other energy products
- Crude oil

(b) Imports by Product

Legend:
- Other products
- Vehicles and transport equipment
- Electrical, electronic equipment
- Mechanical machinery and equipment
- Iron and steel and articles thereof
- Chemical products and plastics
- Energy products
- Agrifood products

(c) Exports by Country

Legend:
- Other countries
- Uzbekistan
- Switzerland
- Republic of Korea
- Russian Federation
- People's Republic of China
- European Union

(d) Imports by Country

Legend:
- Other countries
- Uzbekistan
- Republic of Korea
- United States
- People's Republic of China
- European Union
- Russian Federation

USD = United States dollar.
Source: United Nations Comtrade. International Trade Statistics. https://comtrade.un.org/pb/ (accessed 8 June 2020).

8.   The key destinations for services export are the same—the PRC, the EU, and the Russian Federation, along with Uzbekistan. Services are imported from the same three countries, but also from the Republic of Korea and the US.

9.   In 2010, the role of services export in the economy increased as its share in the GDP grew—from 2.8% in 2010 to 4.9% in 2018. The share of services imports in the GDP was fluctuating in the range of 6.7%–9.7% and accounting for 8.0% in 2018.

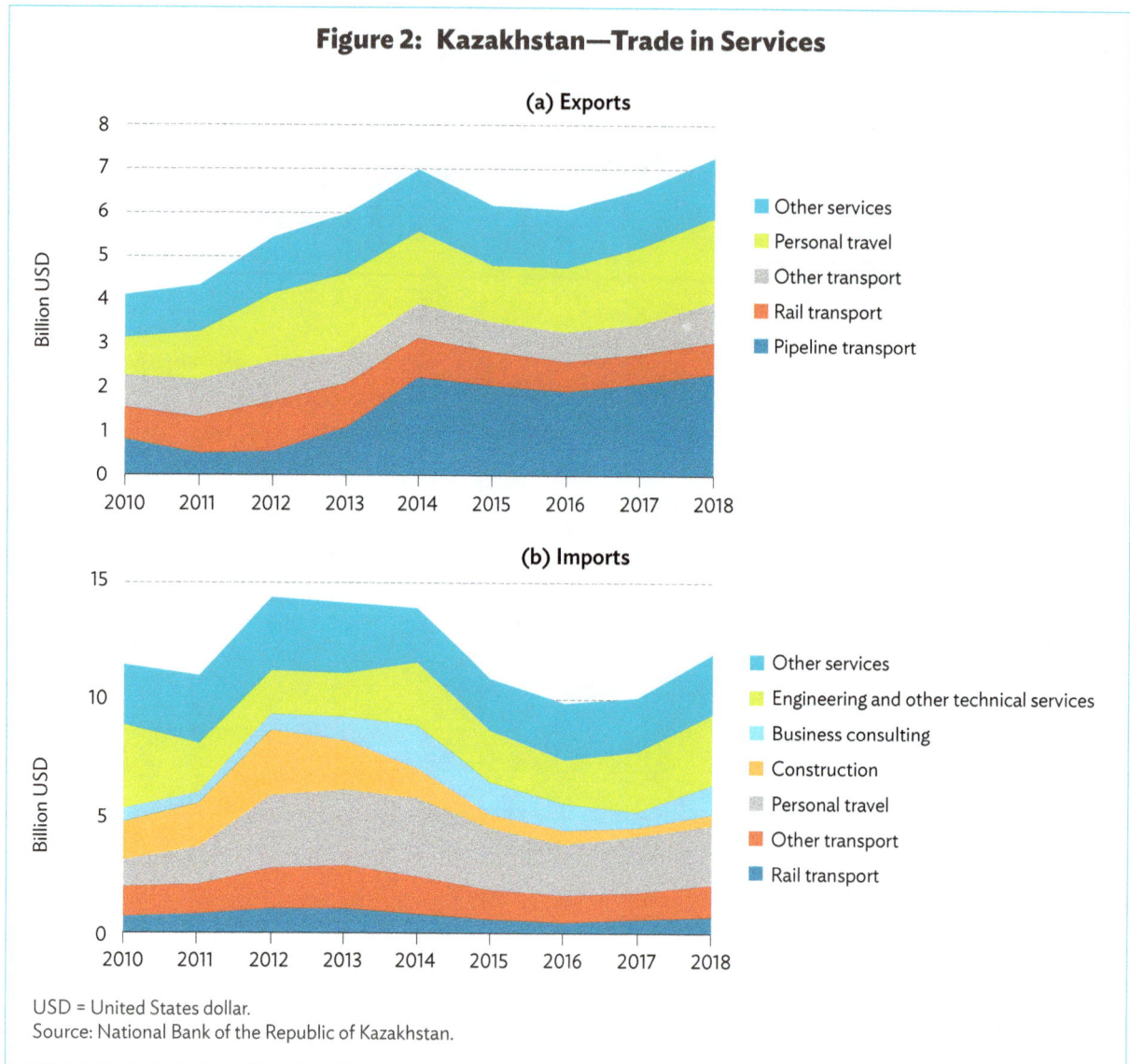

Figure 2: Kazakhstan—Trade in Services

(a) Exports

Legend:
- Other services
- Personal travel
- Other transport
- Rail transport
- Pipeline transport

(b) Imports

Legend:
- Other services
- Engineering and other technical services
- Business consulting
- Construction
- Personal travel
- Other transport
- Rail transport

USD = United States dollar.
Source: National Bank of the Republic of Kazakhstan.

2.2. Tajikistan

2.2.1. Trade in Goods

10. The exports of Tajikistan demonstrated unstable dynamics, mostly due to the decline in its two largest export items: aluminum[1] and raw cotton (Figures 3). These were partially replaced by ores and concentrates of nonferrous metals and by nonmonetary gold.[2] The rise in the share of new export items is a result of the PRC's foreign direct investment in the mining sector of Tajikistan. Tajikistan's imports are much higher than exports with the trade deficit financed by remittances of Tajik workers abroad.[3] Key imported items include agrifood products, energy, machinery and equipment, metals for construction, and consumer goods.

11. The main export destinations for products from Tajikistan are Turkey (aluminum), Kazakhstan and Uzbekistan (ores and concentrates of nonferrous metals), and Switzerland (gold). The key origins of the imports are the PRC, Kazakhstan, and the Russian Federation. Tajikistan also has significant trade with its other neighbors—Afghanistan, Iran, and the Kyrgyz Republic.

12. The dynamics of merchandise exports as a percentage of GDP in 2010 was U-shaped: it had the highest level in 2010 (21.2%), then it fell to just 10.7% in 2014, and then recovered to 17.1% in 2018. It was a result of the changes in the composition of key export products (para. 10). The share of imports in GDP had a declining trend—from 47%–50% during 2010–2014 to 39%–42% during 2017-2018.

---

[1] Exports of aluminum as a commodity were partially reclassified as exports of services (see the next section).

[2] The 2018 gold exports in the official statistics of the country are shown to be zero, so far. However Switzerland (a traditional gold export destination) reported gold imports of $212.1 million from Tajikistan in 2018. As gold exports may be included in Tajikistan's published official report later, the calculations in this section account for the value provided by Switzerland.

[3] The main destination of the Tajik migration is the Russian Federation, and the migrants' remittances are very much dependent on the situation in the oil-dependent Russian Federation economy. This is why Tajikistan imports appear dependent on international energy prices even though Tajikistan is a net importer of oil and gas.

Figure 3: Tajikistan—Merchandise Trade

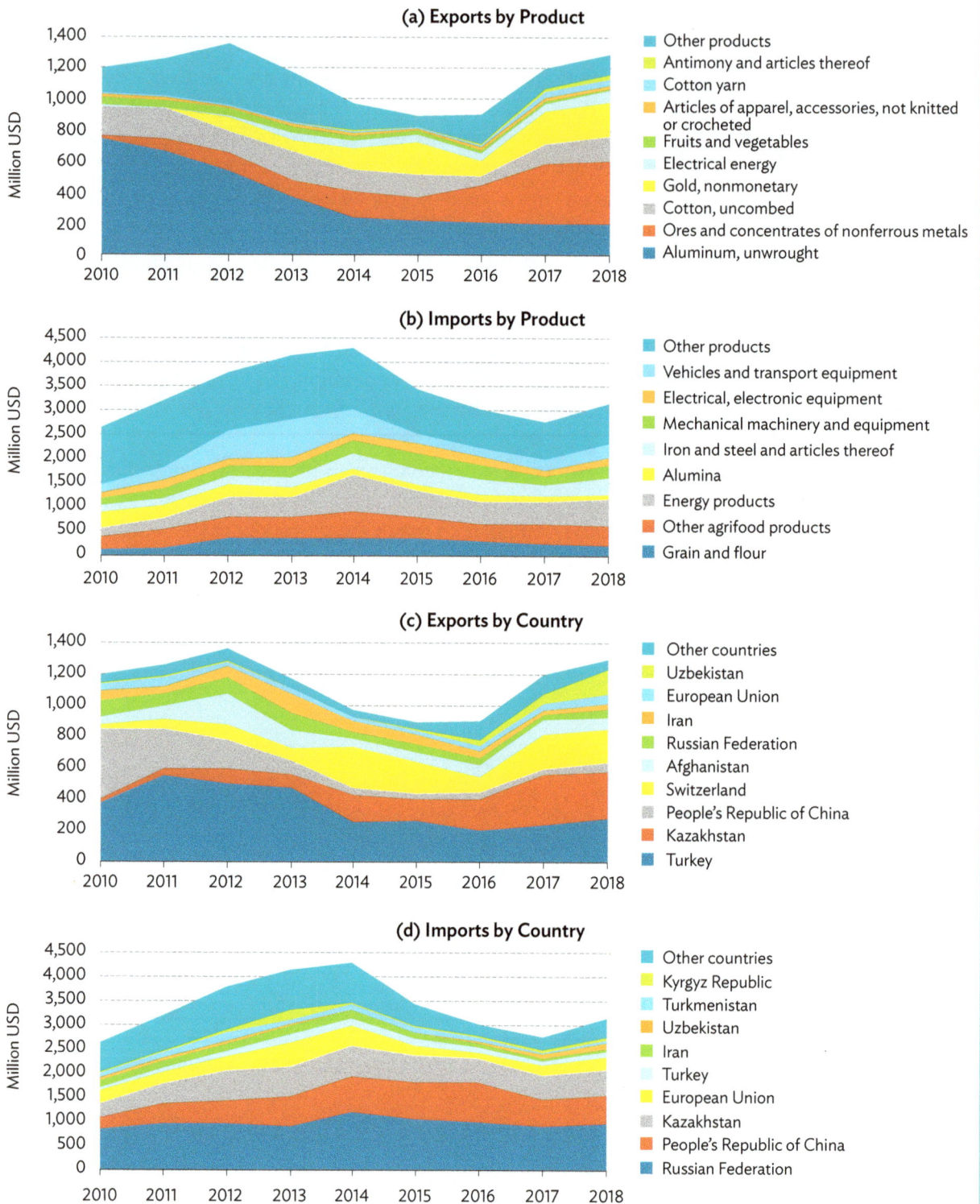

(a) Exports by Product

Legend:
- Other products
- Antimony and articles thereof
- Cotton yarn
- Articles of apparel, accessories, not knitted or crocheted
- Fruits and vegetables
- Electrical energy
- Gold, nonmonetary
- Cotton, uncombed
- Ores and concentrates of nonferrous metals
- Aluminum, unwrought

(b) Imports by Product

Legend:
- Other products
- Vehicles and transport equipment
- Electrical, electronic equipment
- Mechanical machinery and equipment
- Iron and steel and articles thereof
- Alumina
- Energy products
- Other agrifood products
- Grain and flour

(c) Exports by Country

Legend:
- Other countries
- Uzbekistan
- European Union
- Iran
- Russian Federation
- Afghanistan
- Switzerland
- People's Republic of China
- Kazakhstan
- Turkey

(d) Imports by Country

Legend:
- Other countries
- Kyrgyz Republic
- Turkmenistan
- Uzbekistan
- Iran
- Turkey
- European Union
- Kazakhstan
- People's Republic of China
- Russian Federation

USD = United States dollar.
Source: Customs Service of the Government of the Republic of Tajikistan.

2.2.2. Trade in Services

13.   The export of services is important in Tajikistan, providing revenues equivalent to more than 20% of the export of goods (Figures 4a to 4b). The exports, however, were halved between 2012 and 2017. This is due to the reduced export of aluminum smelting services (less than 20% of total services export in 2017 compared to almost half of the total services export in 2010) and some decline in the export of air transport services. Imports consist of services in air transport (37%), construction (34%), and other services (29%) for 2017. The decline in both exports and imports of air transport services during 2015–2017 was due to a contraction in labor migrant flows to the Russian Federation.

14.   The main destinations of services export are the Russian Federation (mostly related to labor migration) and United Kingdom–Anguilla (aluminum smelting). The key origins of imported services are the Russian Federation (also migration-related), the PRC (construction), and other countries.

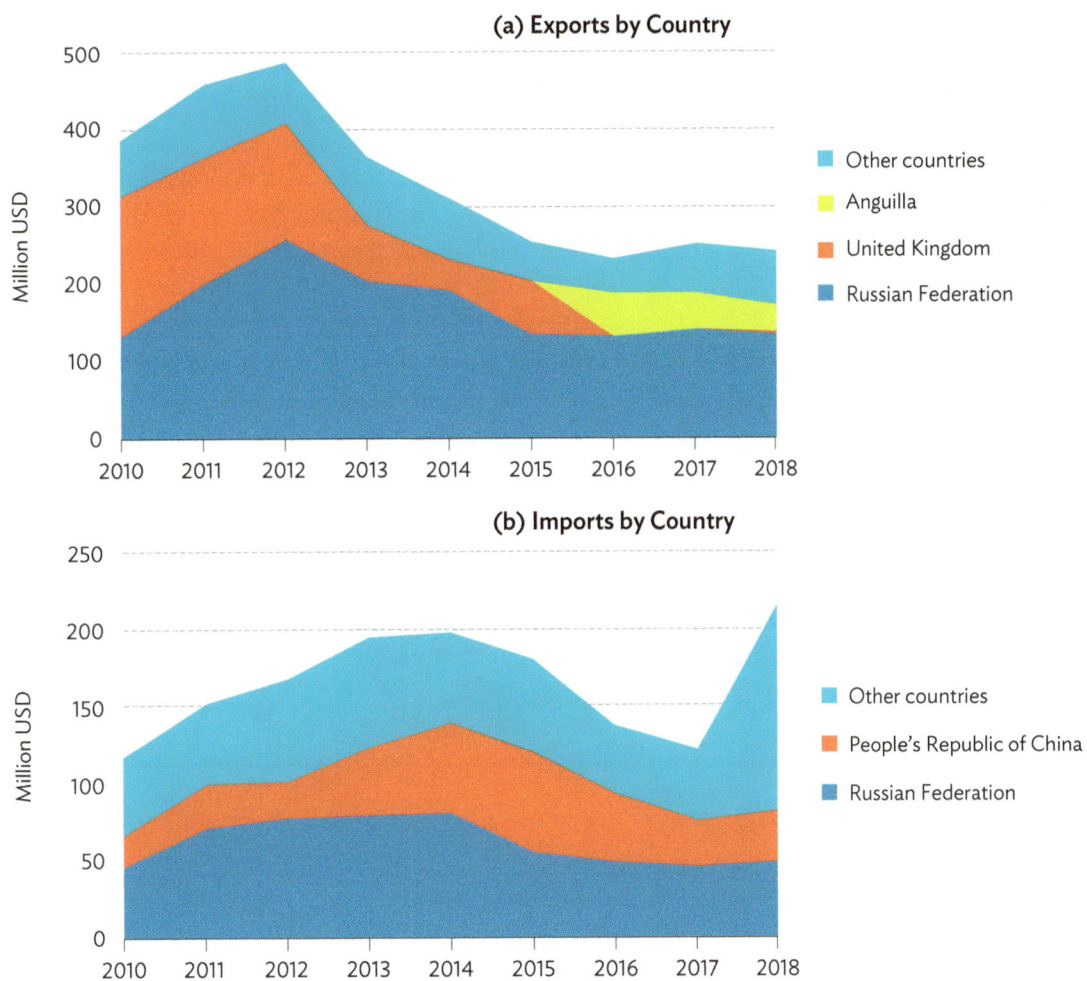

Figure 4: Tajikistan—Trade in Services

USD = United States dollar.
Source: Agency on Statistics under the President of the Republic of Tajikistan.

15.   The drivers of change in the export and import of services mentioned in para. 13 explain the shrinking share of services export in the GDP—from 6.8%–7.0% during 2010–2011 to 3.2% in 2018. The import of services changed without any clear trend, in the range of 1.7%–2.8% of GDP during 2010–2018.

2.3   Uzbekistan

2.3.1. Trade in Goods

16.   Similar to Kazakhstan and Tajikistan, Uzbekistan's exports stagnated in 2010 (Figures 5a to 5e), affected by unfavorable price dynamics for its main export products—gold and natural gas. In line with the new economic policy direction, the government changed its approach to two previously dominating export items. These are (i) uncombed cotton (in line with the policy direction: Reduction of land area under cotton and gradual replacement of raw cotton exports with exports of cotton yarn and some other deeper processed textile products) and (ii) passenger cars (in line with the policy direction: Reduction of implicit subsides for the car-making sector). Instead, vegetables, fruits, and other agrifood products are becoming the key agricultural exports of the country. Since 2012, the merchandise imports of Uzbekistan exceed the exports with growing trade deficit. A substantial part of imports is due to capital and intermediate goods (machinery, equipment, metals, and car components).

17.   The main export destinations of Uzbekistan goods are Switzerland (gold), the PRC (natural gas and other products), and the Russian Federation (natural gas, vegetables, and fruits). The Russian Federation and the PRC, together with the EU and the Republic of Korea, are also main partners for imports.

18.   Both merchandise exports and imports of the country were declining as a percentage of GDP during 2010–2016: from 25% (2010) to 11% (2016) for exports, and from 19% (2010) to 14% (2016) for imports. These flows, however, grew very fast during 2017–2018, achieving the level of 22% of GDP for exports and a record high of 34% of GDP for imports. Such dynamics in the last 2 years were driven not only by the changes in total value of exports and imports, but also by the new exchange rate policy of Uzbekistan, implying a dramatic liberalization of foreign currency transactions. As a result, the official exchange rate was adjusted to equilibrium level.[4] A by-product of this change was the reduction in the dollar value of GDP and an increase in the importance of exports and imports in the economy, as reflected in the GDP shares provided above.

---

4   The average exchange rate changed from SUM2,965/$1 in 2016 to SUM8,070/$1 in 2018.

Figure 5: Uzbekistan—Merchandise Trade

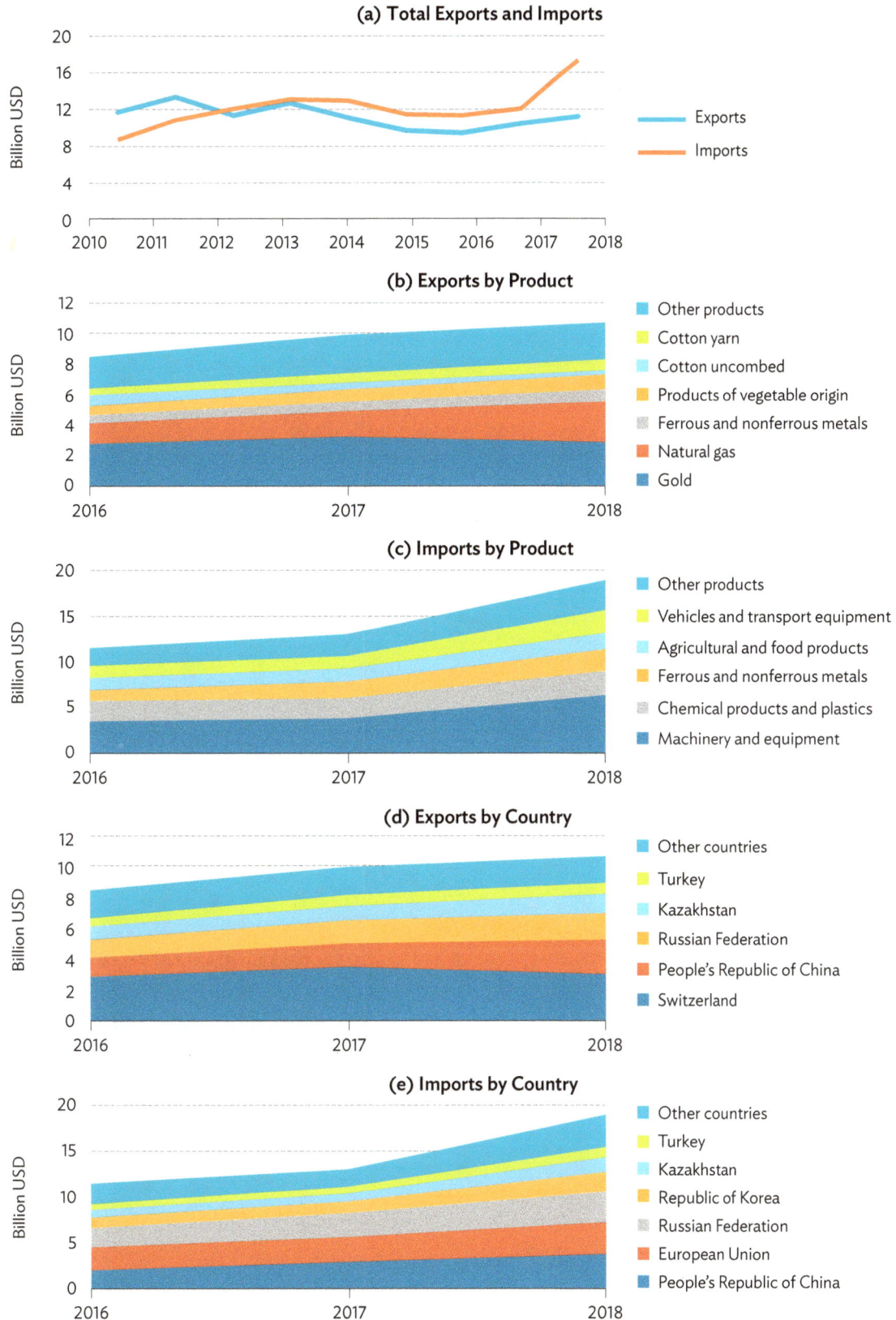

(a) Total Exports and Imports

Exports
Imports

(b) Exports by Product

- Other products
- Cotton yarn
- Cotton uncombed
- Products of vegetable origin
- Ferrous and nonferrous metals
- Natural gas
- Gold

(c) Imports by Product

- Other products
- Vehicles and transport equipment
- Agricultural and food products
- Ferrous and nonferrous metals
- Chemical products and plastics
- Machinery and equipment

(d) Exports by Country

- Other countries
- Turkey
- Kazakhstan
- Russian Federation
- People's Republic of China
- Switzerland

(e) Imports by Country

- Other countries
- Turkey
- Kazakhstan
- Republic of Korea
- Russian Federation
- European Union
- People's Republic of China

USD = United States dollar.
Source: Central Bank of the Republic of Uzbekistan.

2.3.2. Trade in Services

19.   Trade in services (Figures 6a to 6c) is growing in importance for Uzbekistan with exports achieving 24% of total merchandise exports, and imports accounting for 30% of total merchandise imports (2018). The main exported services are personal travel (tourism) and pipeline transport (for the transit of natural gas from Turkmenistan to the PRC). Imported services include transport and personal and business travels.

20.   With the growth in the dollar value of trade in services and the exchange rate dynamics discussed in para. 18, the GDP share of services export increased dramatically from 3% in 2010 to 6% in 2018, while the GDP share of services import also increased from 1% in 2010 to 4% in 2018.

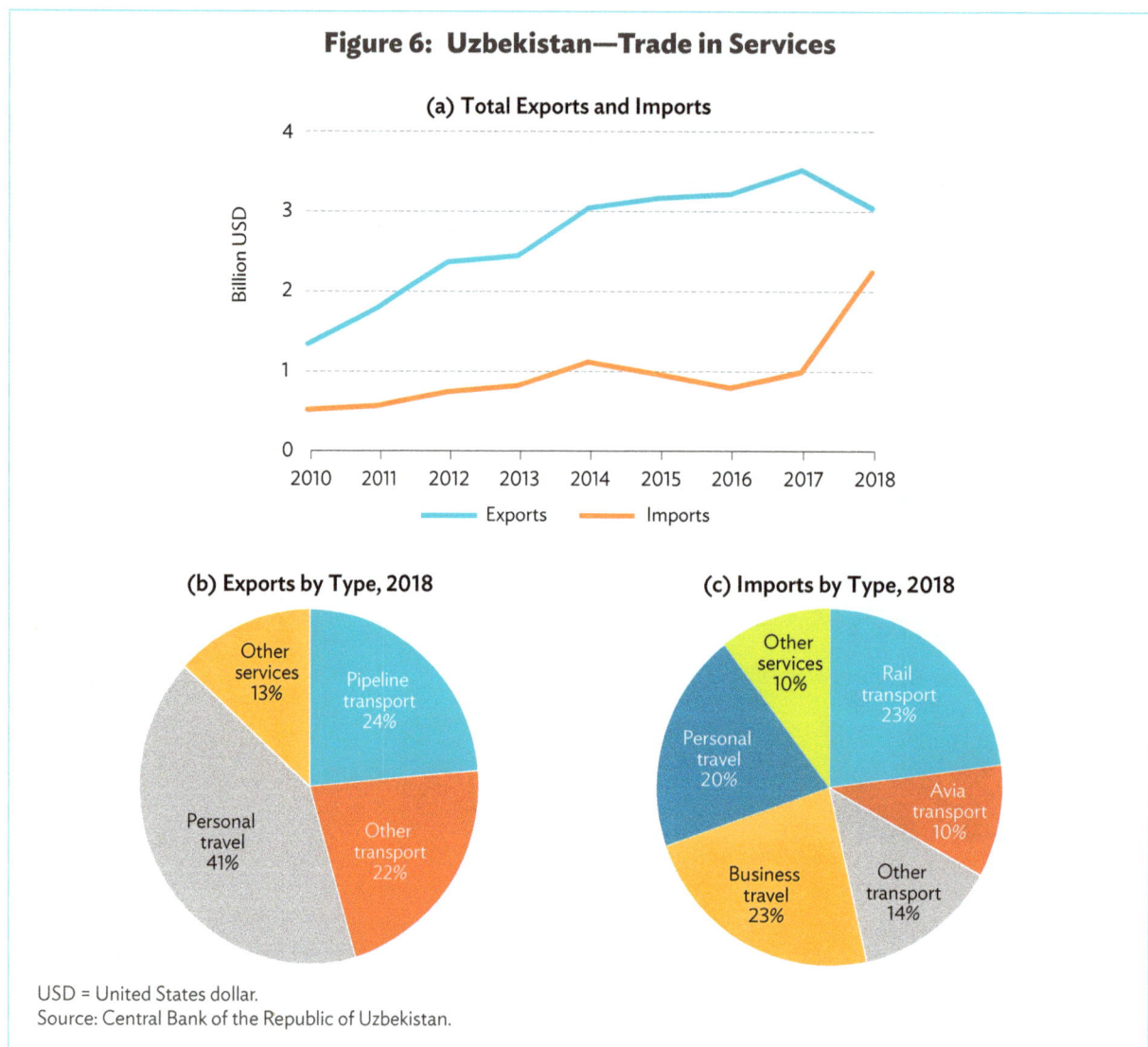

Figure 6: Uzbekistan—Trade in Services

(a) Total Exports and Imports

(b) Exports by Type, 2018

(c) Imports by Type, 2018

USD = United States dollar.
Source: Central Bank of the Republic of Uzbekistan.

2.4.　Trade between Kazakhstan, Tajikistan, and Uzbekistan

21.　During 2010–2018, merchandise trade among the three economies was unstable (Figure 7). Since 2016, trade among these countries picked up and in 2018, it increased by 81% compared to 2016. This is due to the recovery in energy prices, foreign direct investment used in the production of metal ores and concentrates processed in neighboring countries, and policy changes in Uzbekistan. Trade in services is also growing with its total turnover fluctuating at around 30% of the total turnover of merchandise trade. In 2018, the value of trilateral trade in services exceeded $1 billion—based on the data provided by the statistical agencies of these countries.

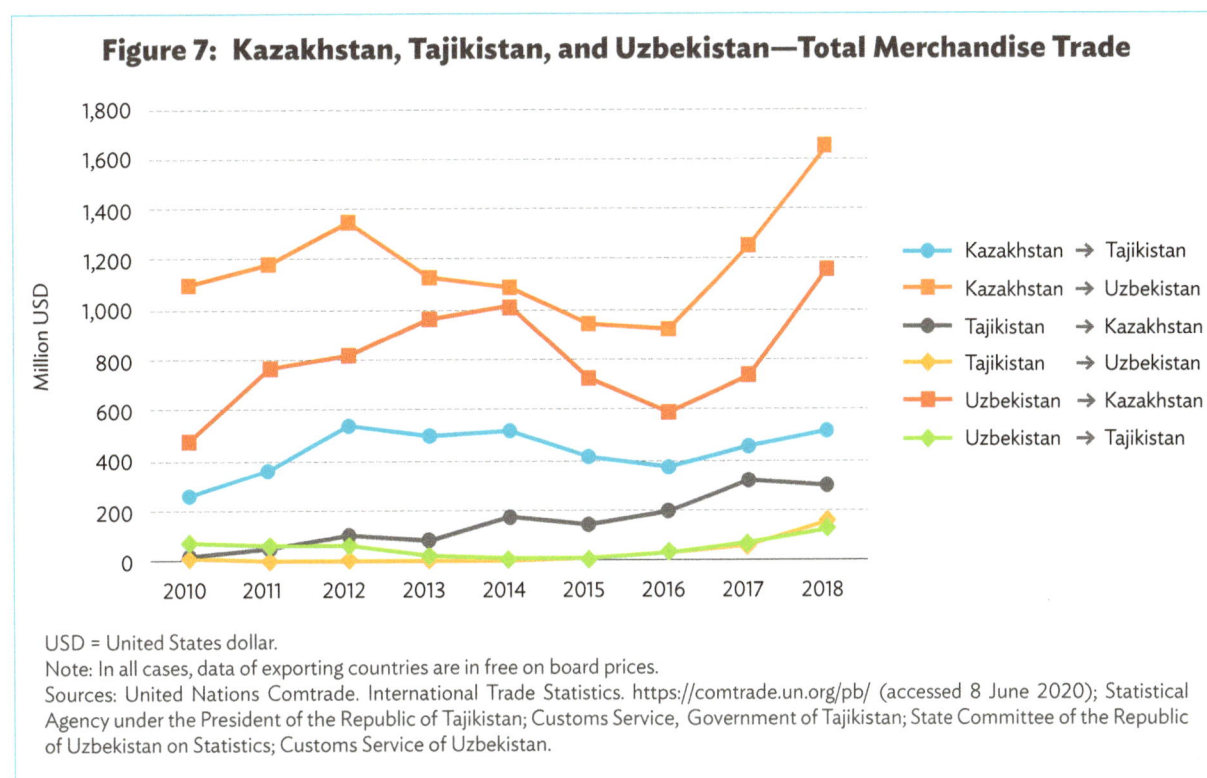

Figure 7:　Kazakhstan, Tajikistan, and Uzbekistan—Total Merchandise Trade

USD = United States dollar.
Note: In all cases, data of exporting countries are in free on board prices.
Sources: United Nations Comtrade. International Trade Statistics. https://comtrade.un.org/pb/ (accessed 8 June 2020); Statistical Agency under the President of the Republic of Tajikistan; Customs Service, Government of Tajikistan; State Committee of the Republic of Uzbekistan on Statistics; Customs Service of Uzbekistan.

22.　Kazakhstan is a major partner for both Tajikistan and Uzbekistan—No. 1 export destination and No. 3 source of imports for Tajikistan, and No. 3 export destination and No. 5 source of imports for Uzbekistan. The main products exported by Kazakhstan to Tajikistan and Uzbekistan include wheat grain and flour, natural gas, steel and iron, and tourism services (Figure 8). Kazakhstan imports nonferrous metals' ores and concentrates[5] from Tajikistan while it imports fruits and vegetables, natural gas, chemicals and plastics, and tourism services from Uzbekistan.

23.　The trade between Tajikistan and Uzbekistan jumped from a meager $12 million in 2015 to $282 million in 2018. For Tajikistan, Uzbekistan is now its No. 4 destination for exports and No. 5 source of imports. For Uzbekistan, Tajikistan is its No. 10 and No. 11 partner for exports and imports, respectively. Tajikistan exports nonferrous metals' ores and concentrates, cement, and electricity to Uzbekistan while Uzbekistan supplies natural gas, nitrogenous fertilizers, and assorted manufactured goods to Tajikistan.

5　The reported imports of fruits and vegetables from Tajikistan have fallen sharply after 2014 (see also section on informal trade below).

Figure 8: Kazakhstan, Tajikistan, and Uzbekistan—Structure of Trade, 2018

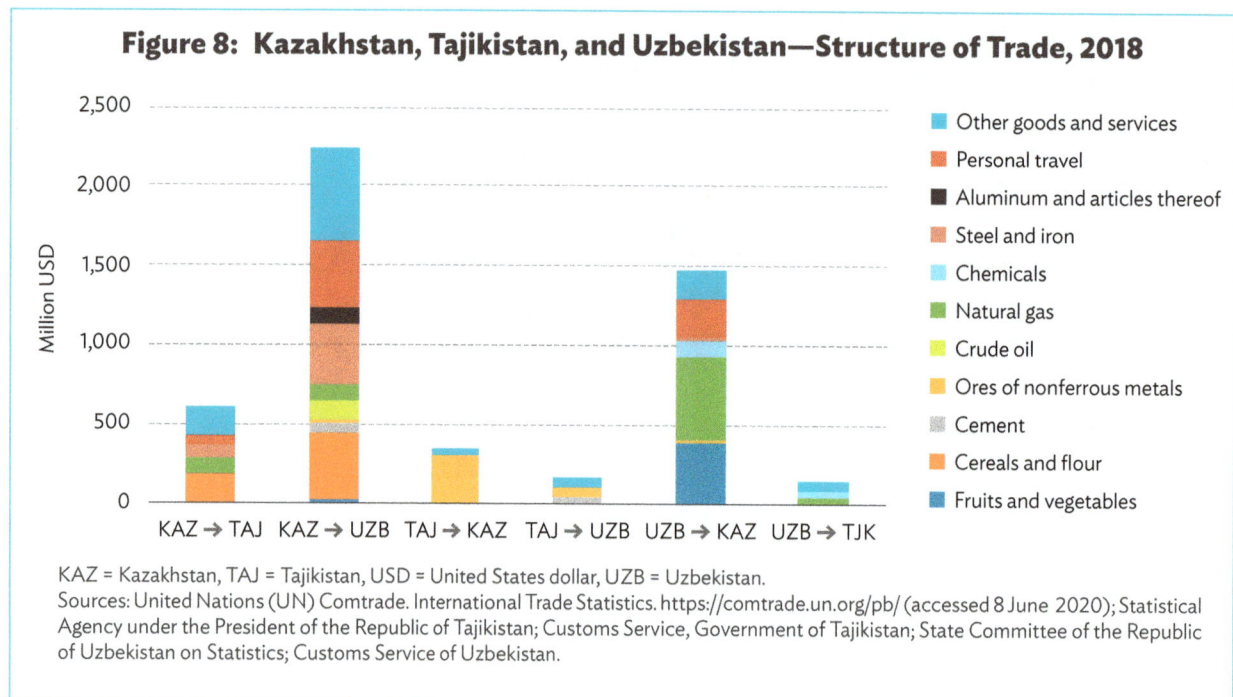

KAZ = Kazakhstan, TAJ = Tajikistan, USD = United States dollar, UZB = Uzbekistan.
Sources: United Nations (UN) Comtrade. International Trade Statistics. https://comtrade.un.org/pb/ (accessed 8 June 2020); Statistical Agency under the President of the Republic of Tajikistan; Customs Service, Government of Tajikistan; State Committee of the Republic of Uzbekistan on Statistics; Customs Service of Uzbekistan.

24.   Thus, one can see a revival of trade in goods and services (mostly tourism and/or personal travel) between these three countries. So far, the trade is concentrated on primary and/or semi-processed products of agriculture, extractive industries, and some manufactured goods and tourism services.

2.5.   Trade within the Shymkent–Tashkent–Khujand Economic Corridor Region

25.   Different parts of the STKEC region are involved in foreign trade at varying extents. Sugd oblast accounts for half of the total merchandise exports and imports of Tajikistan (Figures 9a and 9b). Tashkent city and Tashkent oblast produce more than 20% of Uzbekistan's exports and receive half of the country's imports. The role of Shymkent and Turkestan oblast in the foreign trade of Kazakhstan is relatively small. Sugd oblast in Tajikistan and Tashkent city in Uzbekistan play the roles of import hubs for their respective countries—imported goods arrive there by rail, truck, and air; undergo customs clearance; and then are distributed throughout their respective countries.

26.   Half of Sugd oblast's trade turnover is with Kazakhstan and Uzbekistan (including their non-STKEC parts). Trade with neighbors also constitutes a large part of the foreign trade of Shymkent and Turkestan (Figures 10a and 10b). Most of the trade in Tashkent city and Tashkent oblast are with countries other than Kazakhstan and Tajikistan.

Figure 9: Shymkent–Tashkent–Khujand Economic Corridor Cities and Oblasts—Volume of Trade

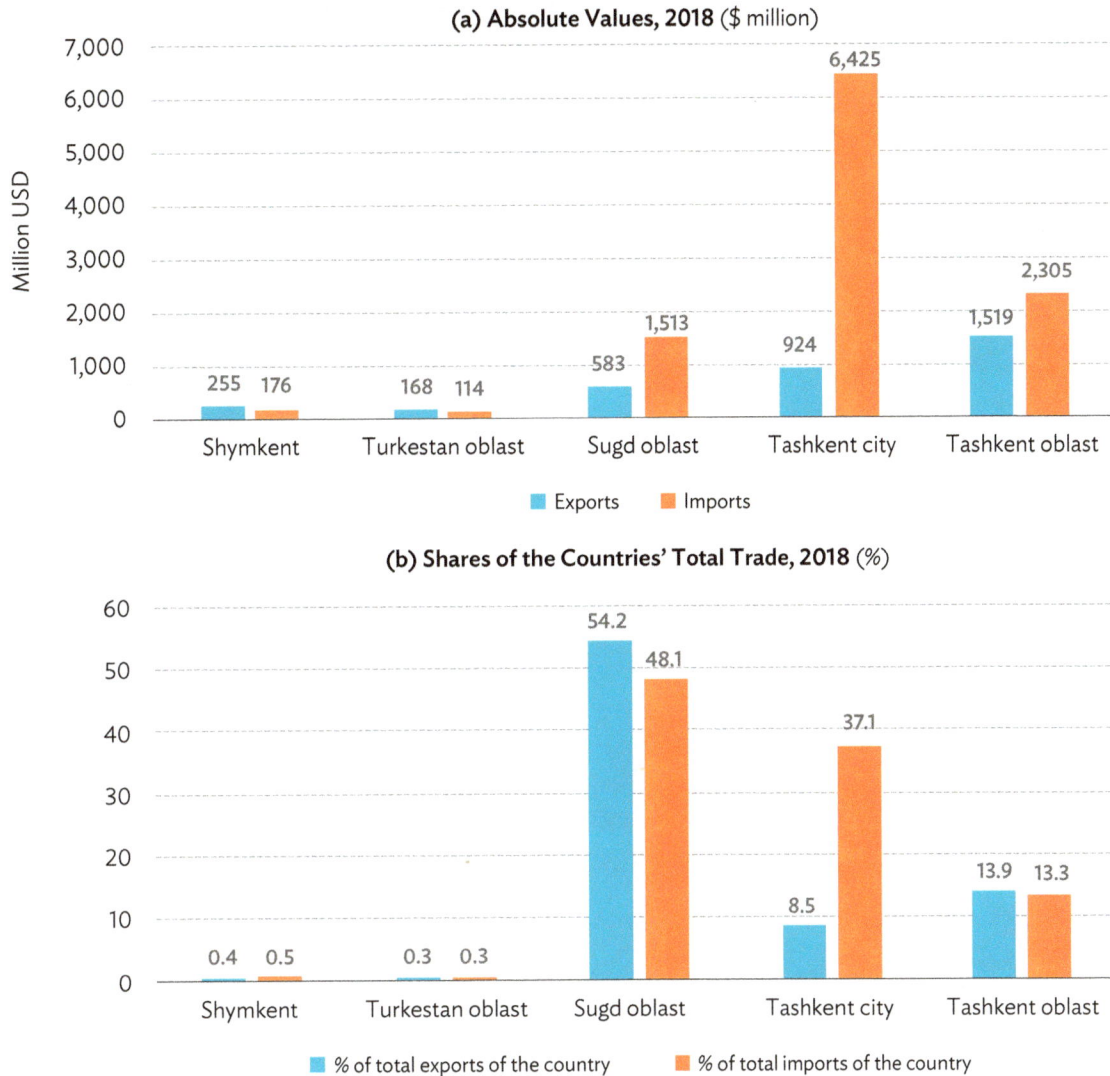

(a) Absolute Values, 2018 ($ million)

(b) Shares of the Countries' Total Trade, 2018 (%)

USD = United States dollar.
Sources: Customs Services of Kazakhstan; Agency of the Republic of Kazakhstan on Statistics; Statistical Agency under the President of the Republic of Tajikistan; Customs Service, Government of Tajikistan; State Committee of the Republic of Uzbekistan on Statistics; Customs Service of Uzbekistan.

Figure 10: Shymkent–Tashkent–Khujand Economic Corridor Cities and Oblasts—Direction of Trade
(%)

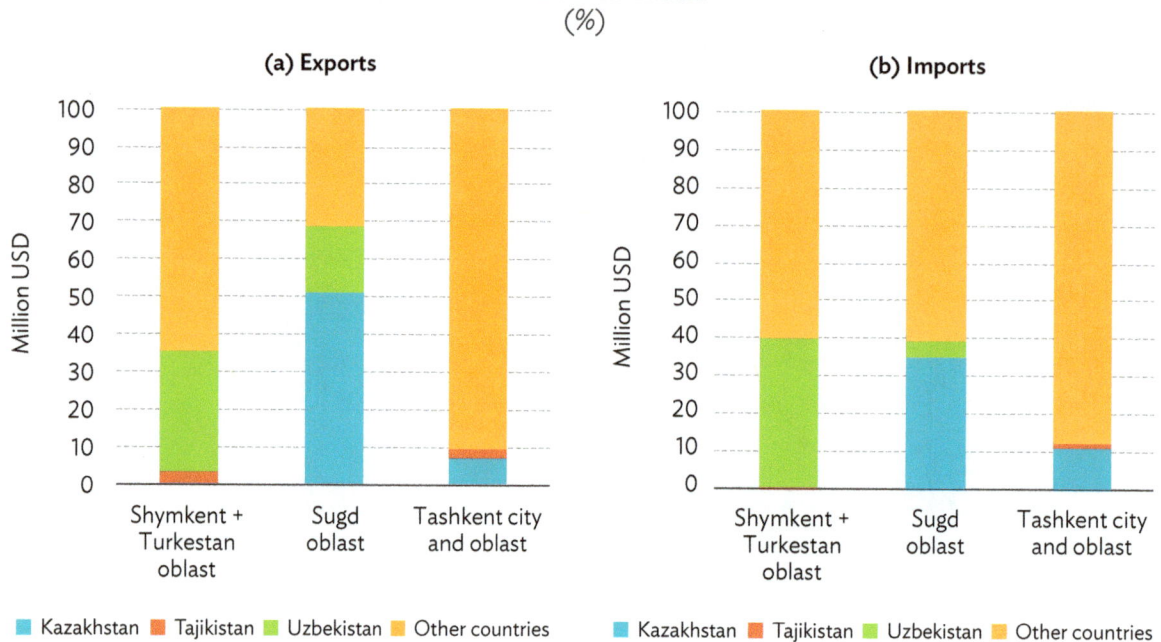

USD = United States dollar.
Sources: Customs Services of Kazakhstan; Agency of the Republic of Kazakhstan on Statistics; Statistical Agency under the President of the Republic of Tajikistan; Customs Service, Government of Tajikistan; State Committee of the Republic of Uzbekistan on Statistics; Customs Service of Uzbekistan.

27.   Exports from all parts of the region generally comprise energy resources (crude oil, oil products, electricity, radioactive elements); ferrous and nonferrous metals and ores; cotton; wheat flour; and manufactured goods such as fertilizers and textiles (Figures 11a to 11e).

28.   Using the approach described in the Appendix, it is possible to assess the total value and product structure of merchandise trade among these three parts of the STKEC region (Table 1 and Figure 12).

Table 1:   Intra-Shymkent–Tashkent–Khujand Economic Corridor Trade
($ million)

	Importer					
	Shymkent + Turkestan oblast[a]	Sugd oblast	Tashkent + Tashkent oblast	Shymkent + Turkestan oblast	Sugd oblast	Tashkent + Tashkent oblast
Exporter	2015			2018		
Shymkent + Turkestan oblast, Kazakhstan		39.2	206.8		14.1	136.1
Sugd oblast, Tajikistan	19.6		2.3	0.9		77.5
Tashkent + Tashkent oblast, Uzbekistan	329.3	1.9		76.4	36.4	

[a]   In 2015, both Shymkent and Turkestan oblasts were part of South Kazakhstan oblast.
Sources: Statistical and customs agencies of Kazakhstan, Tajikistan, and Uzbekistan; author's estimates.

Figure 11: Shymkent–Tashkent–Khujand Economic Corridor Cities and Oblasts—Composition of Exports

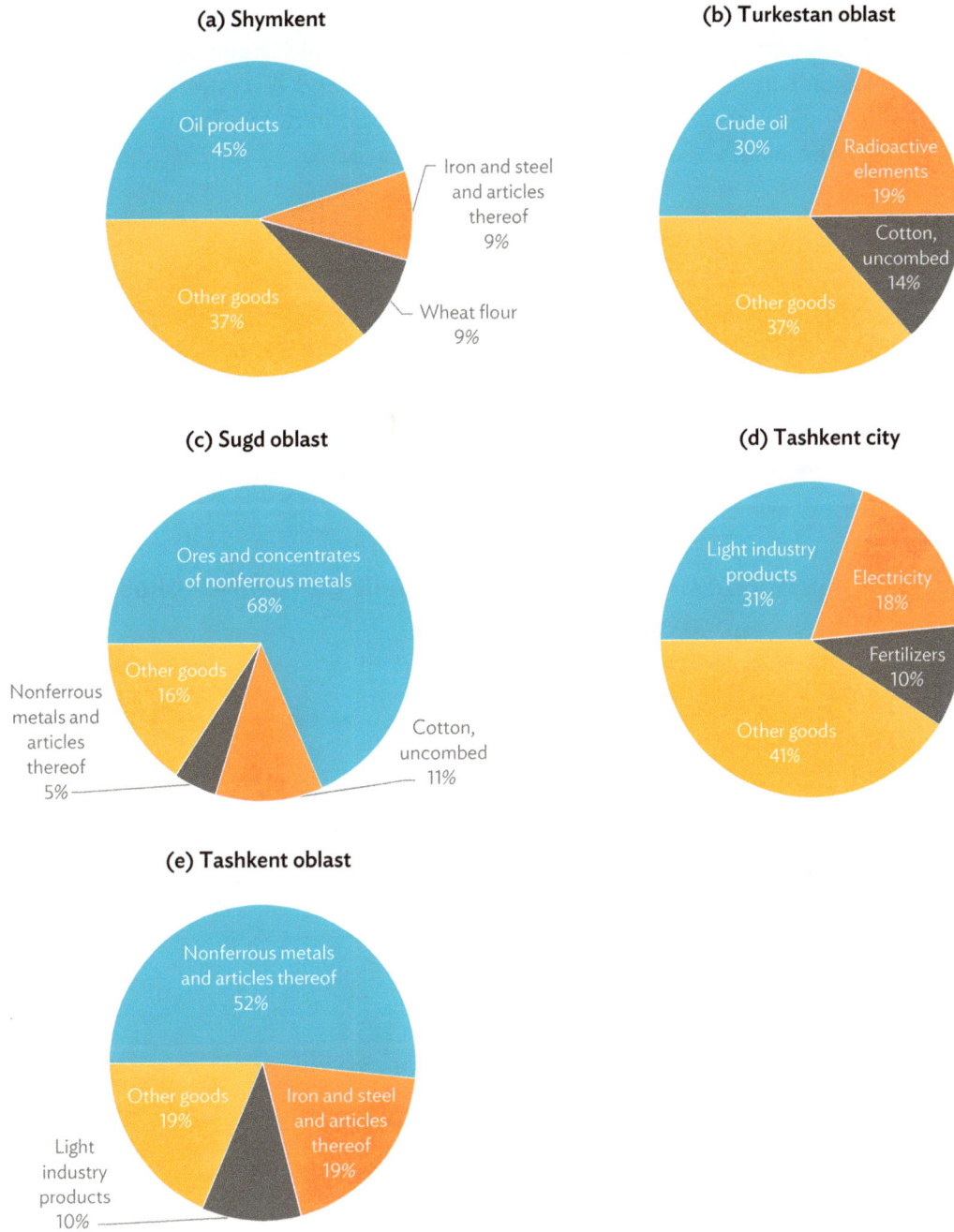

(a) Shymkent

Oil products 45%
Iron and steel and articles thereof 9%
Wheat flour 9%
Other goods 37%

(b) Turkestan oblast

Crude oil 30%
Radioactive elements 19%
Cotton, uncombed 14%
Other goods 37%

(c) Sugd oblast

Ores and concentrates of nonferrous metals 68%
Other goods 16%
Nonferrous metals and articles thereof 5%
Cotton, uncombed 11%

(d) Tashkent city

Light industry products 31%
Electricity 18%
Fertilizers 10%
Other goods 41%

(e) Tashkent oblast

Nonferrous metals and articles thereof 52%
Other goods 19%
Iron and steel and articles thereof 19%
Light industry products 10%

Sources: Customs Services of Kazakhstan; Agency of the Republic of Kazakhstan on Statistics; Statistical Agency under the President of the Republic of Tajikistan; Customs Service, Government of Tajikistan; State Committee of the Republic of Uzbekistan on Statistics; Customs Service of Uzbekistan.

29.   As presented in Table 1, the total merchandise trade turnover within STKEC region in 2015 was $599 million. This is equivalent to 17.3% of the total trade among the three countries or 0.6% of their aggregated trade turnover. This means that the intra-STKEC trade constitutes only a minor part of the total foreign trade of Kazakhstan, Tajikistan, and Uzbekistan. In 2018, the intra-STKEC trade turnover declined to $341.5 million (which accounted for just 7.5% of total trade among the three countries, or 0.3% of their aggregated trade turnover). The trade of Shymkent and Turkestan oblast with Sugd oblast and Tashkent city and oblast fell in both directions, while trade between Tashkent city and Tashkent oblast and Sugd oblast increased dramatically from a very low base.

30.   Consistent with their geographic location in the middle of the STKEC region, Tashkent city and Tashkent oblast account for more than 90% of the intra-STKEC trade. Three main traded products and/or product groups inside the region include (i) zinc ore and concentrate (supplies are from the Tajik–Chinese joint venture Gorprom in Sugd oblast to Almalyk mining and metallurgy plant in Tashkent oblast), (ii) vegetables and fruits from Tashkent oblast to Shymkent and Turkestan oblast, and (iii) wheat grain and flour from Shymkent and Turkestan oblasts to Tashkent city and Tashkent oblast. The second and third items have fallen significantly between 2015 and 2018—trade in these agrifood products between Kazakhstan and Uzbekistan did not change much, it was just reoriented toward other parts of these two countries.

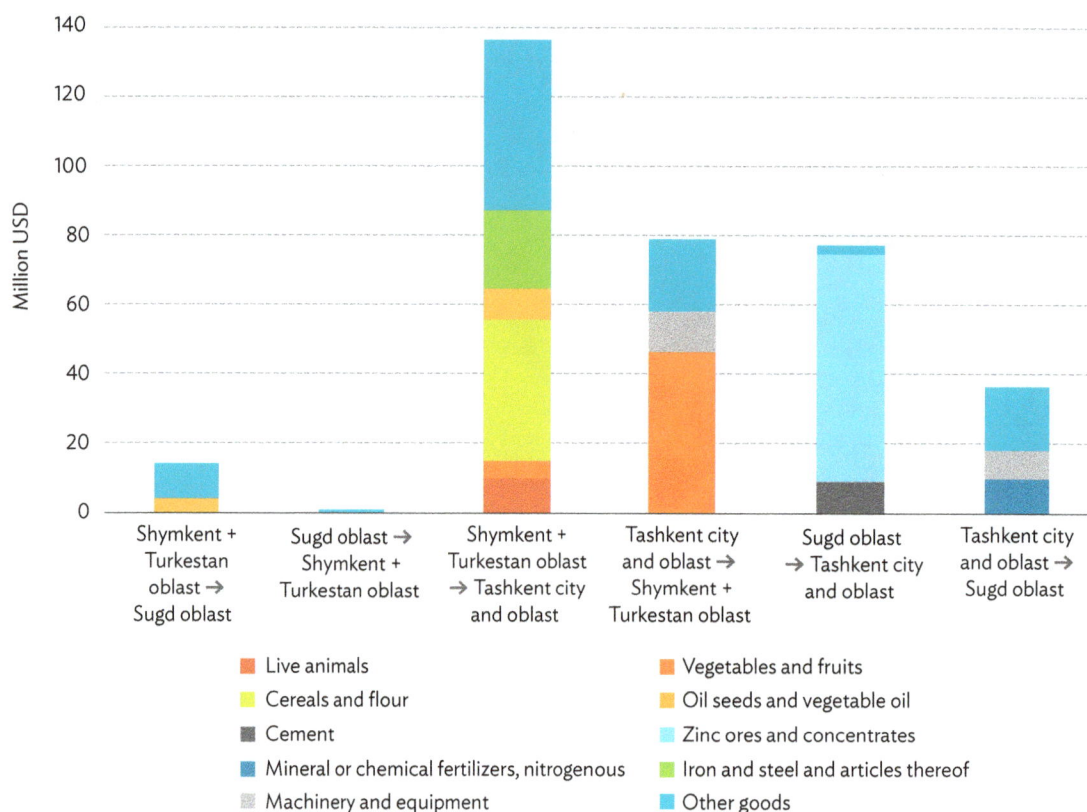

Figure 12: Shymkent-Tashkent-Khujand Economic Corridor—Product Structure of Trade, 2018

USD = United States dollar.
Sources: Customs Services of Kazakhstan; Agency of the Republic of Kazakhstan on Statistics; Statistical Agency under the President of the Republic of Tajikistan; Customs Service, Government of Tajikistan; State Committee of the Republic of Uzbekistan on Statistics; Customs Service of Uzbekistan; author's own estimates.

2.6. Informal Trade in the Countries of the Region

31.   It is well known that official statistics do not fully cover all trade flows in Central Asia, including the STKEC region. Close historical and cultural ties between people on different sides of state borders, porous borders, and governance imperfections in the countries of the region result in significant cross-border flows of goods not registered by official agencies of countries in the region. The motivation for keeping these flows informal varies—ranging from import taxes evasion to attempts to benefit from trade regimes enjoyed by neighboring countries.

32.   Two concrete types of informal flows could be mentioned here. One is the reexport of PRC consumer goods, especially garments and footwear, by individuals from Central Asian countries bordering with the PRC (Kazakhstan, Kyrgyz Republic, and Tajikistan) to countries that have no border with the PRC (e.g., Uzbekistan). In the context of STKEC region, this is mostly flows coming from Kazakhstan to Uzbekistan.[6] It is known that there is a gap worth several billion in US dollars between the PRC-reported values of light industry products' exports from the PRC to Kazakhstan, and Kazakhstan-reported estimates of the same goods' imports (Figure 11a). The difference, most probably, stands for informal imports of these goods to Kazakhstan. These imports are intended partially for the domestic market of Kazakhstan and partially for reexport to neighboring countries, including Uzbekistan. These reexports could easily amount to $0.5 billion–$1.0 billion.

Figure 13: Shymkent-Tashkent-Khujand Economic Corridor—Evidence Suggesting Existence of Informal Trade

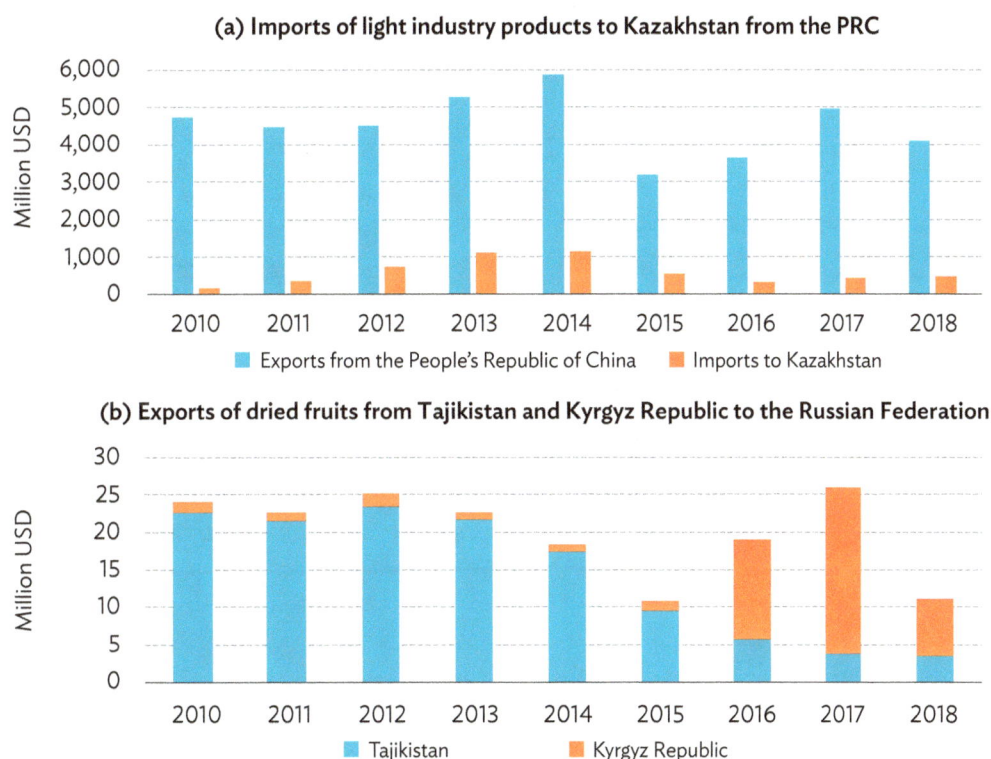

(a) Imports of light industry products to Kazakhstan from the PRC

Exports from the People's Republic of China ■   Imports to Kazakhstan ■

(b) Exports of dried fruits from Tajikistan and Kyrgyz Republic to the Russian Federation

Tajikistan ■   Kyrgyz Republic ■

PRC = People's Republic of China, USD = United States dollar.
Sources: United Nations Comtrade. International Trade Statistics. https://comtrade.un.org/pb/ (accessed 8 June 2020); Customs Service, Government of the Republic of Tajikistan.

---

[6]   A comprehensive discussion of informal trade in Chinese consumer goods in Central Asia can be found in Kaminski and Mitra (2012).

33.   Another type of informal flows is the export of Tajikistan dried fruits (mostly apricots) to the Russian Federation. As Figure 11b suggests, there was a dramatic fall in these exports after 2015, coinciding with a hike in exports of the same product from the neighboring Kyrgyz Republic. Taking into account that the Kyrgyz Republic joined the Eurasian Economic Union (EAEU) in 2015, the most plausible explanation for this unusual change is that Tajikistan fruits are reported to be Kyrgyz Republic fruits in order to enjoy the somewhat simpler regime for trade within EAEU. The scale of this diverted trade flow is in the range of $10 million–$20 million per annum.

2.7.   Transit Trade along the Shymkent–Tashkent–Khujand Economic Corridor

34.   An important function of the STKEC region is to serve the transit of international goods flows by rail and road.[7] The STKEC, especially its part located in Turkestan and Tashkent oblasts, hosts infrastructure that service most of the exports and import goods originating from and/or going to the cities and oblasts of Tajikistan and Uzbekistan—which are not part of the STKEC region. The infrastructure is also used for many flows going to Afghanistan from Kazakhstan, the Russian Federation, and other countries.

35.   The 2018 estimate for transit flows is in the range $23.0 billion ± $2.5 billion. Thus, the transit trade's value is 60–74 times larger than the trade within STKEC region. The implications of this finding are obvious: the transit role of the STKEC should be given a high priority—similar to the importance given to the trade within the STKEC.

2.8.   Trade Outcome Indicators

36.   One could calculate several trade indices, which provide the different characteristics of these countries' trade performance. These characteristics include the (i) intensity of trade with neighboring countries, (ii) degree of the economies' trade structure complementarity, (iii) observable comparative advantages in their exports, and (iv) level of complexity and/or sophistication of the countries' exports.

37.   Trade intensity indices between Kazakhstan, Tajikistan, and Uzbekistan are very high (much more than 1, see Table A2 in the Appendix). This means that these countries trade with each other much more than with other parts of the world. This is a typical situation for neighboring countries.

38.   Trade complementarity indices between Kazakhstan and Uzbekistan (Table A2) are in the range of 20–30, which translates to relatively low complementarity as these countries mostly export goods that are not imported by their partner.

39.   Based on the 2018 data, the revealed comparative advantage indices (RCAIs) for these countries are high (Table A3) for their traditional exports: energy products, metals and ores, raw agricultural produce, some foods, textiles, and chemical products. The only less obvious goods with an RCAI>1 include (i) railway equipment components (HS8605, HS8606, HS8608) for Kazakhstan and Uzbekistan, and (ii) electrical equipment components (HS8535) for Uzbekistan, but the shares of these products in total exports are below 0.1%.

---

[7]   This covers almost all goods, except those transported by pipeline (natural gas) and air (gold and some fruits).

40.   Export sophistication indicators are low, with the export share of high-technology goods being less than 1% of total exports for all three countries (World Bank's World Integrated Trade Solution). The 2018 values of the economic complexity index—another indicator of the technological level of exports—are not high either. For Kazakhstan, the 69th economy out of 137 in the world for which this index was estimated, the value is at –0.046.[8] For Tajikistan, the 109th economy out of 126, based on the data for 2017, the value is at –1.104. For Uzbekistan, the 85th economy out of 137, the value is at –0.47 (The Observatory of Economic Complexity). The product space for the three countries (Figures 14a to 14c) illustrates the points made on the low level of their exports' complexity. The product space can be used to predict future exports, since countries are more likely to start exporting products that are related to current exports. More sophisticated and/or high-technology products are located in the central part of the space; the periphery concentrates simple goods with highly specialized expertise, which is not very helpful in upgrading the export structure. As shown in the figure, most of the products with RCAI values exceeding one (see colored circles on the graphs) in STKEC countries are located on the periphery of the countries' product spaces. This means that it would require an additional effort for them to upgrade their exports (long distance in this space to cover from the current areas of export expertise). The evolution of economic complexity index and product spaces for Kazakhstan, Tajikistan, and Uzbekistan over the last 10–15 years shows no improvement in their economic complexity and in the mix of products with revealed comparative advantages.

41.   As these three economies export mostly primary goods and import mostly manufactured goods, prospects for their intra-regional merchandise trade will very much depend on their progress in developing export-oriented manufacturing. Another obvious direction of export development is the expansion of trade in services, especially tourism and transit transport (for all modes—rail, road, pipeline), which are already picking up. There are also some types of services that are not yet fully traded, so far, but seem to have a natural potential for expansion. These include secondary and tertiary professional education, technologically intensive health care, and others. The expansion of intra-regional trade appears to be an integral part of the general trade upgrading agenda of these three countries. This agenda includes not only the development of trade with neighbors, but also accessing major global and regional markets.

---

8   This index ranges from –2.5 to 2.5 with higher values indicating higher levels of economic complexity.

Figure 14: Kazakhstan, Tajikistan, and Uzbekistan—Product Space

(a) Kazakhstan

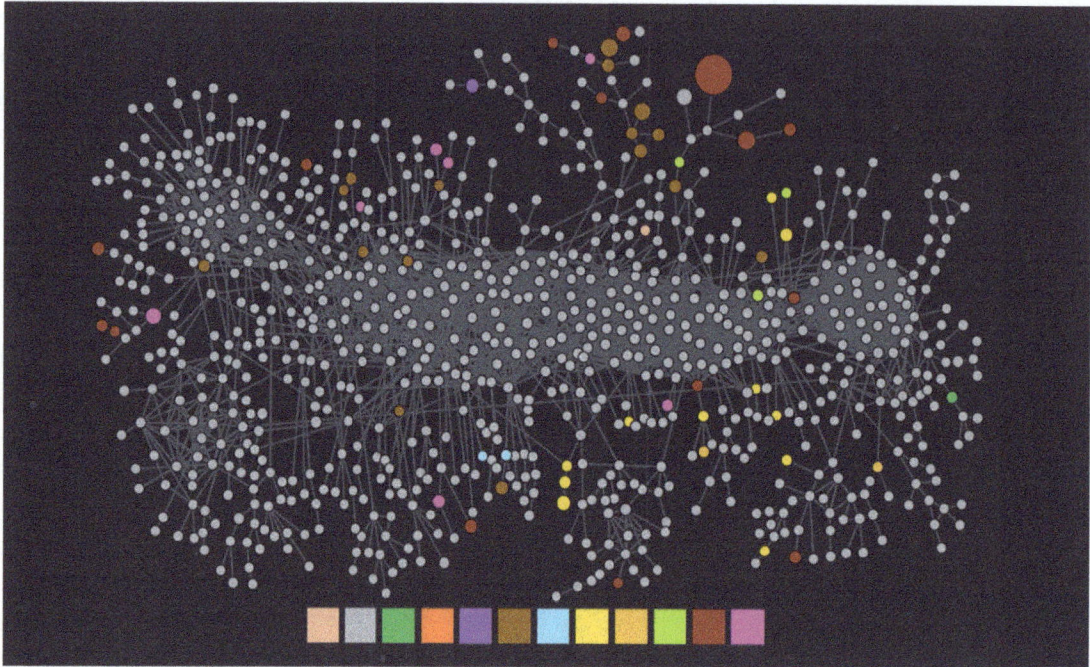

(b) Tajikistan

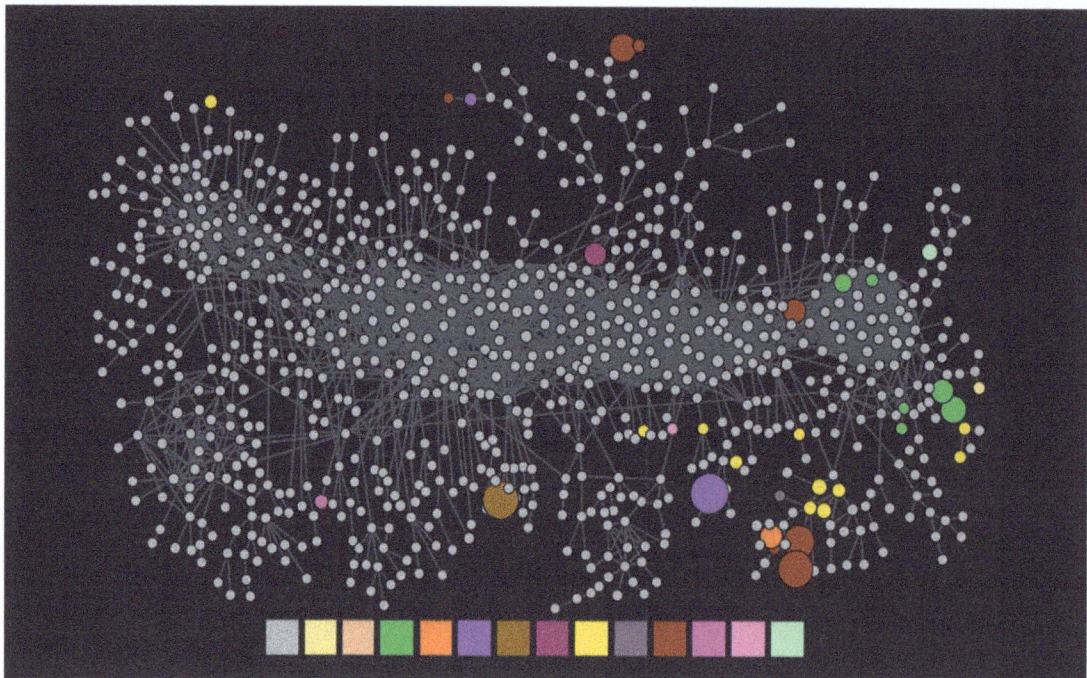

continued on next page

Figure 14 *continued*

(c) Uzbekistan

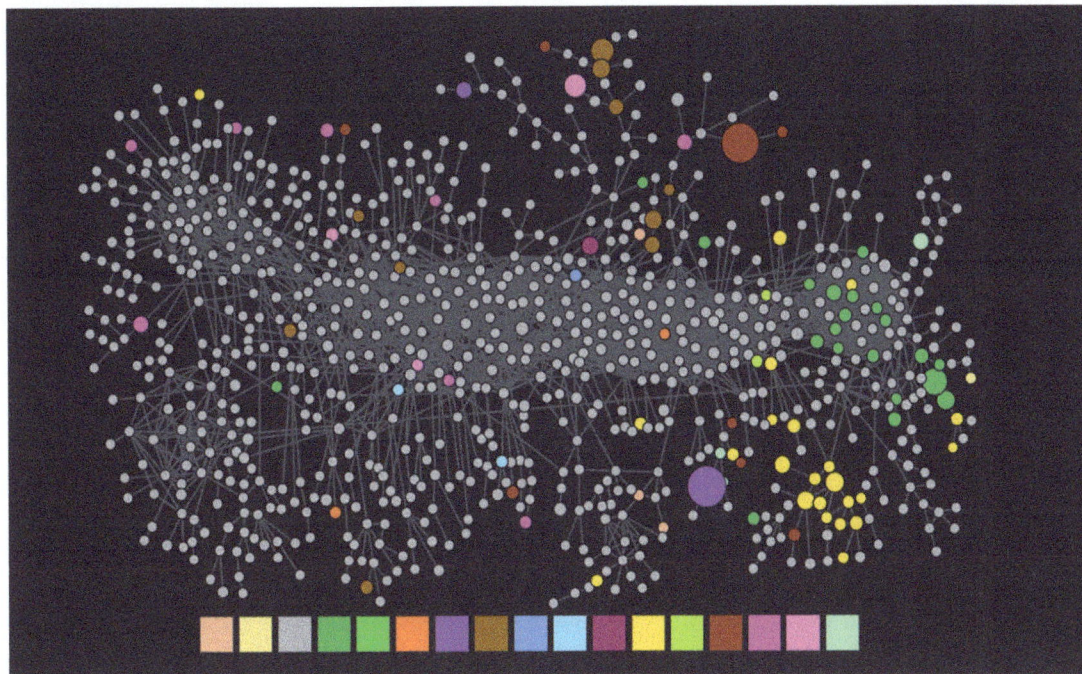

Sources: The Observatory of Economic Complexity. Product Space. https://oec.world/ (accessed 8 June 2020).

3 Trade Regime in Kazakhstan, Tajikistan, and Uzbekistan

42.   **Regime of trade among the three countries.** Kazakhstan, Tajikistan, and Uzbekistan are members of the Commonwealth of Independent States Free Trade Area (CIS FTA).[9] This FTA implies a tariff-free regime of trade among all participating countries (with some exemptions).

43.   Among the countries covered by this paper, Kazakhstan retained the right to impose export duties on supplies of soy beans, sunflower and rape seeds, crude oil, oil products, natural gas, livestock hides and skins, unprocessed wool, ferrous and nonferrous metals scrap, some articles of steel and aluminum, and parts of railway locomotives or rolling stock. Tajikistan has the right to apply export duties to supplies of live animals, chilled meat of bovine animals, vegetables and fruits and their processed products, electricity, animal hides and skins, silk cocoons, wool, cotton, ferrous and nonferrous metals scrap, and articles of aluminum.

44.   Uzbekistan joined the CIS FTA through a separate protocol that allows some exemptions from the standard World Trade Organization (WTO)-consistent trade rules incorporated into the CIS FTA. These exemptions include the following:

(i)   Uzbekistan does not provide *national regime* to other FTA participants. This means that the regime of taxation in Uzbekistan could be different for domestically produced goods and for imported ones. This applies to excise rates for imported products, which are higher than those applied to goods produced within the country. The list of excisable goods for imports is long and includes not only typical products (alcohol, tobacco, oil products), but also goods such as dairy, sugar, confectionery and some processed foods, carpets, articles of steel and aluminum, different mechanical and electrical machines and equipment, vehicles and parts thereof, and lamps and light fittings. Hence, even in the formal absence of import duties inside the CIS FTA, Uzbekistan still has an import-tariff-like policy instrument to regulate trade with its neighboring countries. It is worth noting that current excise rates for goods other than alcohol, tobacco, oil products, and automobiles are moderate in the range of 5%–20%.

(ii)   The country is not going to use CIS Economic Court for dispute resolution.

---

[9]   Other members of CIS FTA include Armenia, Belarus, the Kyrgyz Republic, Moldova, the Russian Federation, and Ukraine.

(iii) Uzbekistan does not apply WTO-consistent rules on subsides, technical barriers to trade and sanitary and phytosanitary measures, payment limitations, value-based customs fees, rules of origin, and the right to apply bans and quantitative restrictions on trade in a broad range of goods[10] (other participants of this FTA sometimes also deviate from these rules, but in general, they have committed themselves to abide by the WTO rules in these regulatory domains).

45.   These exemptions are active either before the date of Uzbekistan's accession to the WTO or until 31 December 2020, whichever date is earlier. As it is unlikely that Uzbekistan joins WTO till the end of 2020, these exemptions will expire in 2021. It remains to be seen if the Government of Uzbekistan just switches to the regular rules of the CIS FTA or negotiates for other trade regime with the countries in this FTA.

46.   **Regime of trade with other countries.** Most favored nation (MFN) import tariffs in all three countries are not very restrictive. The simple average MFN tariff rates are 6.4% in Kazakhstan (2018), 8.1% in Tajikistan (2019), and 8.0% in Uzbekistan (2020). In 2018, Tajikistan increased its import tariffs—the simple average MFN tariff rate went up from 7.7% to 8.1% (WTO final bound rate). In 2019, Uzbekistan also implemented a tariff increase—the simple average MFN tariff rate went up from 5.6% to 8.0%.

47.   Kazakhstan is a WTO member since 2015 while Tajikistan became a member in 2013. Uzbekistan has an observer status at the WTO since 1994.

48.   Kazakhstan is a founding member of the EAEU. This implies free trade area plus single customs territory, customs code, and common customs tariff; and a significant liberalization of labor force movement among member states, single railway tariffs, harmonization of technical requirements to traded goods, and other aspects of trade and economic cooperation among EAEU member countries. Many of these policy areas are now managed by supranational bodies, including the Eurasian Economic Commission (the executive arm of EAEU), EAEU court, and others. Although a member in the EAEU, Kazakhstan's trade regime is different from that of the EAEU. After its WTO accession, the Government of Kazakhstan set an import tariff according to its WTO commitments at levels that are somewhat below the EAEU common customs tariff. The WTO-consistent rates are applied to goods imported under MFN regime for use inside Kazakhstan. A special tracking system is established for goods that enter the EAEU's single customs territory through Kazakhstan's borders but are intended for other EAEU countries. In such cases, the EAEU common customs tariff is applied to these goods.

49.   Tajikistan is also considering the option of an EAEU accession, but no practical actions have been undertaken.

---

10   These include live animals, meat, cereals, flour, vegetable oil, sugar, bread, raw hides, skins and fur skins, silk cocoons, nonferrous metal scraps, and articles of art and antiques.

50.　　Uzbekistan intends to change its trade regime soon. The special arrangements included into the protocol of Uzbekistan's accession to CIS FTA will expire in 2020. A possibility to replace it with a free trade agreement with EAEU is currently discussed. If no other action is taken in 2020, starting from 2021, relationships with non-EAEU CIS FTA member states (Moldova, Tajikistan, and Ukraine) will be regulated by the standard CIS FTA rules. Currently, Uzbekistan is considering two options: (i) WTO accession—negotiations have been relaunched after a long period of inactivity, and (ii) EAEU accession—as a first step, Uzbekistan is now obtaining the observer status at EAEU. Joining both organizations seems a difficult task,[11] and the government would probably choose only one of them.

---

[11]　The tariffs and other trade rules that would be possible to negotiate in the WTO may not coincide with those adopted in the EAEU. It would require a remarkable degree of goodwill from all WTO members, on one hand, and EAEU members, on the other hand, to allow for an option similar to that of Kazakhstan where the country has its own trade regime determined by the WTO commitments (which substantially deviates from the general EAEU trade regime) and still remains a part of the EAEU.

4 Barriers for Trade in the Shymkent–Tashkent–Khujand Economic Corridor Region

51.   According to the World Bank and the United Nations Economic and Social Commission for Asia and the Pacific estimates, trade costs among the three countries are very high at 80%–120% of the costs of traded goods (Table 2).[12] These costs did not change much between 2005 and 2015 despite the impressive economic growth of these economies during this period and the improvements in transport infrastructure due to the massive investments after 2005. It is also noteworthy that in

Table 2: Trade Costs (Share in value of traded goods, %)

Reporting Country	Partner Country	Sector	2005	2015
Kazakhstan	Tajikistan	Agriculture	97.9	82.5
		Manufacturing	102.4	124.8*
		Total trade	95.0	89.3
Kazakhstan	Uzbekistan	Agriculture	143.9	78.2
		Manufacturing	69.9	93.2
		Total trade	88.6	86.9
Kazakhstan	People's Republic of China	Total trade	85.3	87.9*
Kazakhstan	Russian Federation	Total trade	60.1	66.3
Kazakhstan	Turkey	Total trade	121.4	108.8
Tajikistan	People's Republic of China	Total Trade	195.8	178.2*
Tajikistan	Russian Federation	Total trade	106.9	112.7
Tajikistan	Turkey	Total trade	142.4	104.5
Uzbekistan	People's Republic of China	Total trade	135.8	131.5*
Uzbekistan	Russian Federation	Total trade	78.7	99.4
Uzbekistan	Turkey	Total trade	118.5	111.7
For reference:				
Malaysia	Thailand	Total trade	40.8	46.0
Czech Republic	Poland	Total trade	56.8	13.5
Austria	Germany	Total trade	28.8	29.9

Notes: (i) Asterisk * means average for 2011–2013 (used when 2015 data were not reported).
            (ii) No data was reported for costs of trade between Tajikistan and Uzbekistan.
Source: ESCAP-World Bank. *International Trade Costs Database.* https://databank.worldbank.org/source/escap-world-bank:-international-trade-costs# (accessed 8 June 2020).

---

[12]   The bilateral measure of trade costs featured in this database is comprehensive as it includes all costs involved in exporting and importing goods internationally (i.e., bilaterally) relative to those involved in trading goods domestically (i.e., intra-nationally). It captures trade costs in its wider sense, including not only international transport costs and tariffs but also other trade cost components, such as direct and indirect costs associated with differences in languages, currencies, and the cumbersome import or export procedures (adopted from ESCAP-WB Trade Cost Database: Explanatory Note for Users, 2017).

some cases, the cost of trade with the Russian Federation and the PRC are of the same order or lower than the cost of trade with their closest neighbors, which are the STKEC countries. Also, the trade cost among these countries in Central Asia are much higher than the costs typical for neighboring countries in Central Europe (10%–50%) and in the Association of Southeast Asian Nations countries (30%–50%, Table 2). These comparisons imply that trade costs in Central Asia are unusually high—even if there are very few tariff (or tariff-like as the import excise in Uzbekistan) barriers in trade among them and transport costs could not be very high since it requires only short distances to conduct trade among Kazakhstan, Tajikistan, and Uzbekistan.

52.   Several factors are inflating the trade costs in Central Asia. One of these is the "trade diversion" effects created by regional trade agreements (e.g., EAEU, see the dried fruits example in the section on informal trade). Another is the significant difference (about 20%) in railway tariffs for shipments inside EAEU vs. shipments from or to countries outside EAEU. This incentivizes Tajik and Uzbek traders aiming to export their produce to the Russian Federation and/or northern Kazakhstan to sell their goods to their counterparts in Shymkent and/or Turkestan oblast (the entry point to EAEU) to save on transport costs. Such difference in tariffs may be high for goods with relatively low price-to-weight ratios, as in the case of fresh vegetables and fruits where transport can cost up to 15%–30% of the value of goods. It is well known that trade diversion results in efficiency losses, which translate into increased trade costs. In this case, the diversion implies use of the services of intermediaries in the Kyrgyz Republic side (for Tajikistan dried fruits) or Kazakhstan side (for railway tariffs for Tajikistan and Uzbekistan goods) who do these for fees. Hence, export operations become less profitable for Tajik and Uzbek producers as trade costs tend to increase.

53.   Another important and persistent factor is "imperfect business processes and governance issues" during border crossing and transport of goods across the territories of Central Asian countries and in some of their neighbors. This includes long processing time of trucks and trains when crossing intercountry borders due to infrastructure issues, inefficient organization of the process, cumbersome paperwork, the necessity for truck drivers to make side payments on the borders and on their way, and others. These issues were already known for quite some time (ADB 2006), but progress to improve these is still very modest. To monitor the situation, ADB, in cooperation with freight-forwarding associations in the Central Asia Regional Economic Cooperation (CAREC) countries, established the CAREC Corridor Performance Measurement and Monitoring (CPMM) system. Figure 15 provides data on the key trade facilitation indicators measured along all six CAREC corridors. One can see that 7 out of 10 (5 for road and 5 for rail) indicators did not sustainably improve nor deteriorate in 2019 in comparison to 2010. Some progress was registered for *time taken to clear a BCP* for rail transport and for *speed without delay to travel on the corridors* for both road and rail transport. The latter indicator may reflect the infrastructure improvements, which were fully neutralized by the delays along the way (no improvements recorded for *speed with delay*). This underscores the fact that infrastructure per se is only a part of the problem. The bigger issue is the way transport and border clearance processes in CAREC countries were inefficiently organized. These findings seem relevant not only for CAREC corridors in general, but also for their segments belonging to the STKEC region. While no sufficiently systematic data on the CPMM indicator values related to this region are available, selected indicators' time series portray very similar picture (Table 3). While some improvements were registered at border crossing points (BCPs) Keles (rail, inbound) for *time*, and Fotehobod (road, outbound) and Oibek (road, outbound) for *cost*, the performance of other BCPs or the same BCPs serving the flows going in the opposite direction either worsened, or remained at the same level in 2019 as in 2010. For

STKEC countries, CPMM researchers recommended (i) developing new economic corridors including the STKEC, (ii) increasing the efficiency of BCPs, (iii) removing customs escort for shipments using Transports Internationaux Routiers (TIR), and (iv) enhancing wagon supply, among other things (ADB 2020a).

Figure 15: Corridor Performance Measurement and Monitoring Indicators

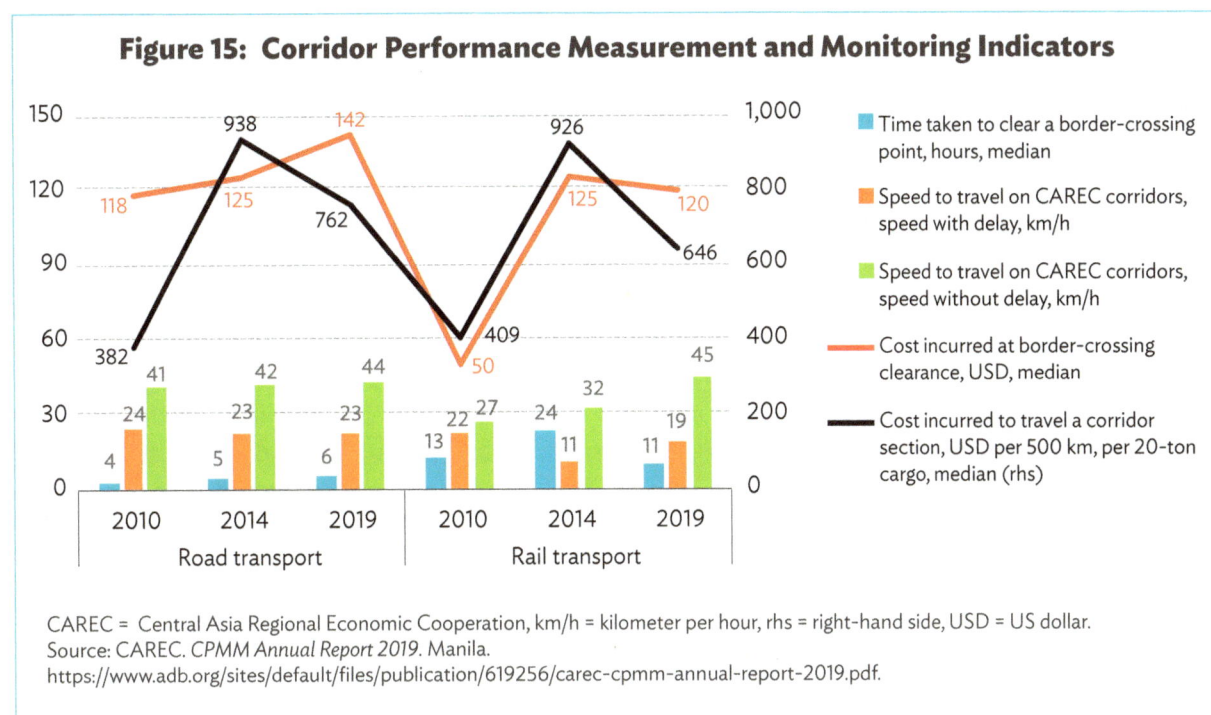

CAREC = Central Asia Regional Economic Cooperation, km/h = kilometer per hour, rhs = right-hand side, USD = US dollar.
Source: CAREC. *CPMM Annual Report 2019*. Manila.
https://www.adb.org/sites/default/files/publication/619256/carec-cpmm-annual-report-2019.pdf.

Table 3: Shymkent–Tashkent–Khujand Economic Corridor—Selected Corridor Performance Measurement and Monitoring Indicators

BCP	2010	2014	2019
Time taken to clear a border crossing point, hours			
Saryagash, Kazakhstan, rail (outbound)	5.0	3.6[a]	9.6
Keles, Uzbekistan, rail (inbound)	n/a	4.9[a]	2.4
Oibek, Uzbekistan, road (outbound)	4.5	4.2	1.3
Fotehobod, Tajikistan, road (inbound)	8.0	6.6	1.9
Cost incurred at border crossing clearance, $			
Keles, Uzbekistan, rail (inbound)	n/a	71b	119
Oibek, Uzbekistan, road (outbound)	160[b]	81	15[c]
Fotehobod, Tajikistan, road (outbound)	80[d]	n/a	27[c]
Fotehobod, Tajikistan, road (inbound)	74	79	476

BCP = border crossing point, n/a = not applicable.
[a] Data for 2013.
[b] Data for 2012.
[c] Data for 2018.
[d] Data for 2011.
Source: Excerpts from the Corridor Performance Measurement and Monitoring database provided by ADB.

54.   World Bank's *Doing Business* study points in the same direction. In the latest version of *Doing Business 2020*, Kazakhstan is ranked 105, Tajikistan at 141, and Uzbekistan at 152 out of 190 on the component "Trading across borders." This is a major improvement when compared to their ranks on the same component in *Doing Business 2010* (with Kazakhstan ranked 182, Tajikistan at 179, and Uzbekistan at 174). At the same time, however, all these ranks are way below the aggregate ranks these countries have in *Doing Business*, e.g., in the 2020 edition, these aggregate ranks were 25 for Kazakhstan, 106 for Tajikistan, and 69 for Uzbekistan. Thus, the time and cost to export and import, when measured by this component in the *Doing Business*, are the most problematic areas of business environment in these economies.

55.   Other factors contributing to the high trade costs include suboptimal physical infrastructure (automobile roads and railways, BCPs, quality testing and certification, among others) and structural issues. An extensive literature exists on transport and other infrastructure in CAREC region (see CAREC Transport Strategy 2030). The joint infrastructure for quality assurance appears to be one of the areas that did not yet receive enough attention. The countries of the region do not seem to have sufficient number and variety of laboratories to test potential export products for compliance with importing countries' technical requirements, sanitary and phytosanitary measures, and other certification regulations. Infrastructure development is a big agenda, which seems beyond the scope of this report. However, from trade costs perspective, it is important to make sure that these compliance costs are not too high. In the current situation, the costs are high because the export values are not sufficiently large to make these costs tolerable for exporters. Thus, economy of scale is one of the issues these economies face (see also the next para.). One way to reduce these costs is to develop regional infrastructure (laboratories, legislation, and certification processes for compliance assurance), which would be in demand by exporters of every country in the region as long as they have similar export structure (i.e., all of them have big export potential of agricultural goods and, hence, need similar types of assurance). Providing this type of regional public goods may become one of the ways to use the STKEC. A related type of regional public good is developing a common definition and certification process for organic production. Organic food (especially vegetables and fruits) is one of the high value-added product types in which the region has an obvious comparative advantage. The exceptional quality and reasonable cost of these produce originating from southern Kazakhstan, Tajikistan, and Uzbekistan are well-known in the former Soviet Union states and, increasingly, beyond. However, some investments are necessary to (i) establish proper certification, which is needed in assigning the organic produce the status recognizable by potential premium export markets; and (ii) maintain the supply of inputs required for this kind of production, among others. While individual countries are already trying to address these issues by themselves, regional cooperation may significantly reduce the costs and improve the efficiency of such investments.

56.   The development of human capital is an important type of regional public goods in the STKEC region. All these countries, at varying extents, experience an acute need of professionals capable of advancing export-oriented businesses. These include agricultural extension experts; engineers in the fields of agrifood processing, mining, and metallurgy; medical workers; and logistics and tourism professionals, among others. This list is just indicative and not exhaustive. Providing quality secondary and tertiary professional education implies high fixed costs (e.g., investments in quality technical colleges and universities), but are worth sharing among the countries of the region. This would require (i) a common design of the education system, (ii) harmonization of education standards and legislation (e.g., licensing requirements and education quality assurance systems) in at least some sectors of the

economy, and (iii) finding a fair allocation of such educational establishments to different parts of the STKEC region. If this lack of domestic human capital is not addressed, the only way would be to import this expertise from abroad. Reliance on foreign professionals is obviously a much more expensive option, hence, this further increases trade costs in the region.

57.	On structural issues, these include asymmetric trade flows, lack of economies of scale, financing and currency exchange operations, and business practices, which all tend to inflate trade costs. As noted earlier in this report, these countries tend to export primary goods and import processed products. This means that for transport, different types of equipment (e.g., uncovered vs. covered wagons) or even different modes should be used (e.g., pipelines or refrigerated trucks for exports, and railway transport and non-refrigerated trucks for imports). This implies that on their return trip, some transport equipment could be in idle mode, yet such costs are already integrated into the transport cost for the sender. For the transport operator to avoid idle runs, it needs to wait and spend some time to consolidate cargo for inbound/outbound shipments, but this will require additional costs. Some of the exporters and/or importers lack economies of scale and may not be able to consolidate sufficiently large consignment. For this reason, they incur higher transport costs. The cost of financing is generally high in Tajikistan and Uzbekistan. A typical interest rate for loans at national currency in 2019 was 25% per annum (in both countries). It is cheaper in Kazakhstan at 12%–15% per annum in 2019. Uzbekistan's exchange rate issue was significantly alleviated when the country unified its exchange rate in 2017 and allowed for virtually unlimited currency conversion on current account transactions. However, the dependence of these economies on international energy and on other commodity prices resulted in the high vulnerability of their currencies' exchange rates.[13] Such dependence also introduces significant exchange rate risks to all transactions in foreign currency, and this is yet another factor that increases trade costs. Some of these structural issues could be addressed only with time and massive investments. Some issues also relate to the general economic policies of the three governments and do not seem to be part of the economic corridor development agenda.

---

[13]	A recent episode of this vulnerability is the depreciation of the Kazakh tenge—ffrom T1/$382.5 on 10 March 2020 to T1/$448.5 on 20 March 2020. The currency lost 15% of its value in just 10 days. By 2 June 2020, however, it has already appreciated to T1/$408.61 (source of data: National Bank of the Republic of Kazakhstan).

5 Potential for Trade in Shymkent–Tashkent–Khujand Economic Corridor

58.   All countries in the region aim to diversify their export products and markets, and the STKEC development provides vast opportunities for achieving this. To be internationally competitive in the production of manufactured goods (other than the traditional ones) and be capable of offering services for exports, the companies in the region need to be exposed to domestic and regional competition. It is also easier to start the export of higher-value-added products (which is the goal of the export diversification efforts) to neighboring countries than to distant ones. For this kind of goods and services, a major challenge is to identify and sustain the demand of loyal consumers abroad. Consumer interest and loyalty seem much easier to gain in other countries of the STKEC: the brands are recognizable, the consumers' tastes are better known or understood, and advertisement campaigns could be much more targeted and cheaper. Also, transport and other costs are lower due to the shorter distance compared to other potential export destinations, especially if some of the trade-cost-inflating issues discussed in the previous section are addressed. Thus, the STKEC region may be considered as a "laboratory" for export product development. If this first step in export upgrade and expansion is successfully accomplished, it could serve as a platform for the expansion of trade and exports to more distant but also more capacious and lucrative markets, such as the PRC, Europe, Japan, and others.

59.   There are also some areas for development among the nontraditional tradeable products aiming for intra-STKEC market, especially in services. Some types of human-, financial- and capital-intensive services require large markets and/or economies of scale to become commercially viable. These services include (i) quality secondary and tertiary professional education, (ii) technologically intensive health care, (iii) culture and entertainment, and (iv) recreational weekend tourism, among others. The language and cultural proximity of the societies in the STKEC region is a major advantage that can be capitalized on. Every part of the corridor has its own unique area or "jewels" as destinations for cultural and recreational tourism for regional visitors. These include historical (Penjikent) and religious (Turkestan) centers, places for skiing (Chimgan), beach resorts (Kairakkum reservoir), and others. Tashkent, the largest city in Central Asia, is naturally positioned to be a regional center in education, health care, and research. Mutuality is the key in developing these services as regional businesses. It would require increased investments, not only in facilities and equipment, but more importantly in human capital, institutional harmonization, liberalizing the cross-border mobility of people, and other "soft" types of infrastructure and resources. This dimension of STKEC development may provide the largest economic, social, and political payoffs in the long term.

60.   Another important reason for expecting trade increase in the STKEC region is the possibility of regional value chains development. An important lesson that the coronavirus disease (COVID-19) pandemic is teaching everybody is the need to increase the resilience of supply and/or value chains due to the possibilities of border closures and other types of disruptions. The risks of such disruptions

seem to grow very quickly with geographic distance between chain links and the number of borders to be crossed. From this perspective, regional value chains have chances to be more reliable than global ones, that is, if all STKEC governments consider these regional chains as a priority and something to hone and protect.

61.   Export diversification is expected to be reflected in the growth of intraregional trade. Taking into account that many structural issues in trade (section 4) are similar in all countries of the region, the provision of regional public goods that address the common structural issues could be conducive to increasing exports—both inside and outside the region.

62.   Projections on the future growth of trade within the region are provided below. These are based on the assumption of a very fast expansion of the intra-regional trade as observed in the last several years. This intra-regional trade growth so far was mostly based on its recovery from very low levels—due to the remarkable lack of regional cooperation in the previous period of development. In the near future, however, this recovery is expected to be accompanied by growth arising from improvements related to STKEC development. The forecasting methodology of trade flows until 2030 is described in the annex.

63.   Due to the general economic growth[14] and proportional expansion of exports and imports, trade among the three countries and transit trade along the STKEC are going to increase by 35% in 2025 and by 65% in 2030 in comparison to 2018 levels. Also, due to (i) investments in the STKEC's transport connectivity and infrastructure for quality assurance, (ii) the development of agrifood and other value chains, and (iii) the streamlining of border crossing procedures and other measures, the merchandise trade turnover among the three countries is going to increase—from $3.90 billion in 2018 to $6.84 billion in 2025 and $9.90 billion in 2030 (Table 4).

Table 4: Kazakhstan, Tajikistan, and Uzbekistan—Merchandise Trade
($ million)

Exporter	Importer	2018	2025	2030
Kazakhstan	Tajikistan	520	940	1,360
Kazakhstan	Uzbekistan	1,643	2,590	3,530
Tajikistan	Kazakhstan	300	500	700
Tajikistan	Uzbekistan	155	290	440
Uzbekistan	Kazakhstan	1,155	2,300	3,550
Uzbekistan	Tajikistan	126	220	320
Total		**3,900**	**6,840**	**9,900**
Increase from 2018			75%	154%

Note: These estimates include both the effects of overall economic growth and from economic corridor development.
Source: Author's own estimates.

---

[14]   The assumptions on the average economic growth rates during 2018–2030 are rather conservative in this report—4% per annum for Kazakhstan and 5% per annum for Tajikistan and Uzbekistan. These values are below the long-term growth rates for these countries and too conservative to account for possible negative shocks for growth during this period such as, for example, the COVID-19 pandemic.

64.   The effect of the STKEC development on intra-STKEC trade is expected to be even larger (Table 5). Based on the assumptions of increasing intercountry trade and the growing role of the STKEC areas in this trade (see Appendix for details), the turnover of trade between Shymkent and Turkestan oblast, Sugd oblast and Tashkent city and Tashkent oblast is expected to increase from $0.34 billion in 2018 to $0.79 billion in 2025 and $1.58 billion in 2030.

Table 5: Intra-Shymkent–Tashkent–Khujand Economic Corridor Merchandise Trade
($ million)

Exporter	Importer	2018	2025	2030
Shymkent + Turkestan oblast	Sugd oblast	14	50	110
Shymkent + Turkestan oblast	Tashkent city + oblast	136	320	660
Sugd oblast	Shymkent + Turkestan oblast	1	20	60
Sugd oblast	Tashkent city + oblast	78	140	220
Tashkent city + oblast	Shymkent + Turkestan oblast	76	200	450
Tashkent city + oblast	Sugd oblast	36	60	80
Total		**341**	**790**	**1,580**
Increase to 2018 (%)			**131**	**363**

Source: Author's estimates.

65.   It is also expected that improvements in infrastructure and border crossing procedures will contribute to the growth of transit trade with third countries or among non-STKEC parts of the three countries. This is forecasted to increase from the current $23.0 billion[15] in 2018 to $37.9 billion to 2030.

66.   Another growth area related to the STKEC development is trade in services. This is related to tourism aimed both at visitors from STKEC countries and tourists from other countries. There is also a substantial (yet mostly untapped) potential of trade in education, health, and cultural services within the STKEC region. Based on a linear extrapolation of the service trade growth between Kazakhstan, Tajikistan, and Uzbekistan[16] during 2013–2018, one could expect this trade to increase from $1.04 billion in 2018 to $1.50 billion in 2025, and $1.82 billion in 2030.

---

[15]   The middle of the interval estimate of $23.0 ± 2.5 billion is provided in the section on transit trade.
[16]   No data on trade among cities and/or oblasts is available.

6 Conclusions and Policy Recommendations

67.   The discussions in the previous sections allow the following conclusions:

(i)   Exports of the STKEC countries stagnated for the last several years.

(ii)   Exports are still concentrated on a relatively few and mostly primary goods.

(iii)   Trade within STKEC region is small and not growing.

(iv)   Transit trade is very important.

(v)   Trade in services in the region is underdeveloped.

(vi)   Key barriers to intra-regional trade are on infrastructure, governance issues, organization of border crossing procedures, other trade facilitation issues, and the structure of economies (asymmetrical trade flows, lacking in economies of scale, underdeveloped financial markets, among others) rather than due to narrowly understood trade policy matters.

(vii)   The region has a big potential for trade expansion and sophistication.

68.   The following could be recommended to the governments and business communities of the STKEC region:

(i)   Maintain free trade regime in the region.

(ii)   Provide regional public goods aimed at export expansion and/or diversification, such as
    - joint network of quality certification facilities (e.g., legislation and laboratories);
    - joint development of standards and certification for organic produce; and
    - joint professional education and business development programs for prospective export sectors (e.g., tourism).

(iii)   Promote intra-regional trade in tourism, transit transport, and other types of services to foster such trade; implement institutional harmonization; and develop human capital in the respective areas.

69.   Developing transport and border-crossing infrastructure is important for intra-regional and transit trade, including passenger traffic, which is important for trade in services.

Appendix:
Methodological Notes

Estimation of Intra-Corridor Trade

No direct data on trade among parts of the countries (e.g., between Shymkent and Sugd oblast) is available. However, it is possible to estimate the trade flows within the corridor with some degree of precision. The estimation methodology is possible because both exports and imports in trilateral trade are concentrated on very few products. The available subnational statistical databases in all three countries report the exports to or imports from each of their partner countries by product (at 4-digit Harmonized System [HS] codes). As shown, the export of some products from city/oblast A of one these countries to city/oblast B of the neighboring country could not be higher than (i) the exports reported by A to the whole neighboring country, and (ii) the imports reported by B from the whole country of A. So, the minimum of two values—the reported exports from A to B's country and the reported imports of B from A's country—is considered as an estimate of the product's exports from A to B. For example, in 2018, Shymkent and Turkestan oblasts of Kazakhstan reported exports of cereals and flour to Uzbekistan worth $40.5 million. At the same time, Tashkent city and Tashkent oblast reported imports of cereals and flour of $257 million from Kazakhstan. Then, the export of cereals and flour from Shymkent and Turkestan oblasts to Tashkent city and Tashkent oblast could not exceed $40.5 million, hence, this value is considered as an estimate for this trade flow. This is an upper bound estimate and it is possible that some parts of these exports went to other areas of Uzbekistan. Also, the difference between the free on board (FOB) prices of exports and the cost, insurance, and freight (CIF) prices of imports is considered negligible in this methodology.

Estimation of Transit Flows

Apart from serving the intra-corridor trade, the Shymkent–Tashkent–Khujand Economic Corridor (STKEC)region also serves the following surface[1] trade flows:

- Trade of Shymkent and Turkestan oblasts with non-STKEC parts of Tajikistan and Uzbekistan;
- Trade of Tashkent city, Tashkent oblast, and Sugd oblast with non-STKEC parts of Kazakhstan;
- Part of trade between the non-STKEC parts of Tajikistan and Uzbekistan and their northern, western, and eastern partners globally (another part could be served by rail and automobile roads connecting Tajikistan with Uzbekistan south of Sugd oblast, and Uzbekistan with Kazakhstan and the Kyrgyz Republic west or east of Tashkent oblast);
- Part of trade between Afghanistan and its northern partners (Kazakhstan, the Russian Federation, and other countries using the transport infrastructure connecting Afghanistan with Uzbekistan).

---

[1] Trade relying on air or pipeline transport should be excluded.

Taking this economic geography into account, the merchandise trade transiting through STKEC region could be considered as a sum of the following components:

(i)   Total trade among Kazakhstan, on the one hand, and Tajikistan and Uzbekistan, on the other hand, less intra-STKEC trade;

(ii) Total trade of Tashkent city, Tashkent oblast, and Sugd oblast with other trade partners;

(iii) Part of the trade of non-STKEC regions of Tajikistan and Uzbekistan with their partners on the west, north, and east (except the Kyrgyz Republic and transit flows via the Kyrgyz Republic); and

(iv) Trade between Afghanistan and Kazakhstan and/or the Russian Federation.

This approach implies some estimation errors, e.g., some rather minor part of trade between Kazakhstan, on the one hand, and Tajikistan and Uzbekistan, on the other hand, may go via less populated western oblasts of Kazakhstan and Uzbekistan. Also, some part of Afghanistan imports from Kazakhstan and the Russian Federation may come through the railroad connecting Karakalpakstan (Uzbekistan) and western Kazakhstan, bypassing the STKEC region. However, the main source of uncertainty is the value of the third component above. For the purposes of this report, it is assumed that 50%–90% of total trade between non-STKEC parts of Tajikistan and Uzbekistan, while 50%-90% of the transit trade component involving Afghanistan are served by STKEC region's transport infrastructure. The resulting estimate, hence, is an interval one.

Details of the estimations are provided in Table A1.

Table A1: Estimation of the Value of Merchandise Trade Transiting via Shymkent-Tashkent-Khujand Economic Corridor Region, 2018

Item No.	Component of Trade	Source/Formula	Value, $ million
1	All trade between Kazakhstan, on the one hand, and Tajikistan and Uzbekistan, on the other hand, less intra-STKEC trade	= 2 + 3 – 4	3,364.5
2	Total trade between Kazakhstan and Tajikistan	SCA	819.8
3	Total trade between Kazakhstan and Uzbekistan	SCA	2,886.2
4	Intra-STKEC trade	Table 1	341.5
5	Total trade of Tashkent city, Tashkent oblast, and Sugd oblast with trade partners other than STKEC countries	= 6 – 7	10,939.5
6	Total exports and imports of Tashkent city, Tashkent oblast, and Sugd oblast	SCA	13,269.4
7	Total trade of Tashkent city, Tashkent oblast, and Sugd oblast with STKEC countries	SCA	2,329.9
8	Trade of non-STKEC regions of Tajikistan and Uzbekistan with their partners in the west, north, and east	= 9 – 5 – 10 – 11 – 12 – 13	10,456.9
9	Total exports and imports of Tajikistan and Uzbekistan	SCA	32,451.2

continued on next page

Table A1 *continued*

Item No.	Component of Trade	Source/Formula	Value, $ million
10	Trade with neighbors (Afghanistan, Kazakhstan, the Kyrgyz Republic, Turkmenistan, Tajikistan and/or Uzbekistan)	SCA	5,464.7
11	Trade with partners in the south (Gulf countries, India, Iran, Pakistan)	SCA	810.5
12	Exports of gold (transported by air)	SCA	2,909.5
13	Exports of natural gas (transported by pipeline) except neighboring countries	SCA	1,870.0
14	Trade between Afghanistan and Kazakhstan and the Russian Federation	UN Comtrade	1,909.1
15	Lower-bound estimate of transit trade	= 1 + 5 + 0.5*(8 + 14)	20,487.1
16	Upper-bound estimate of transit trade	= 1 + 5 + 0.9*(8 + 14)	25,433.5

SCA = statistical and customs agencies, STKEC = Shymkent–Tashkent–Khujand Economic Corridor, UN = United Nations.
Source: Statistical and customs agencies of the STKEC countries.

Trade Outcome Indices

The *trade complementarity index* (**TCI**)[2] measures the degree to which the export pattern of country *j* matches the import pattern of another country *i*. It is defined as

$$TCI_{ij} = 100 \left(1 - \frac{1}{2} \sum_k | m_{ik} - x_{jk} | \right),$$

where m_{ik} is the share of good k in total imports of country and i, x_{jk} is the share of good k in total exports of country *j*. **TCI** varies from 0 (no complementarity) to 100 (full complementarity).

The *trade intensity index* (**TII**) is used to determine whether the value of trade between two countries is greater or smaller than would be expected on the basis of their importance in world trade. It is defined as the share of country *i*'s exports going to country *j* divided by the share of world exports going to country *j*:

Thus:

$$TII_{ij} = x_{ij} / x_{wj},$$

where x_{ij} is the share of country *j* in total exports of country and *i*, x_{wj} is the share of country *j* in total world exports. The value of index of more than 1 indicates a bilateral trade flow that is larger than expected, given the partner country's importance in world trade.

[2] The text and formula in this section were adopted from the World Integrated Trade Solution. https://wits.worldbank.org/wits/wits/witshelp/Content/Utilities/e1.trade_indicators.htm (accessed 8 June 2020).

Table A2: Trade Complementarity Index and Trade Intensity Index Values, 2018

Exporter	Importer	Value
TCI		
Kazakhstan	Uzbekistan	22.7
Uzbekistan	Kazakhstan	26.1
TII		
Kazakhstan	Tajikistan	4,401
Kazakhstan	Uzbekistan	2,977
Uzbekistan	Kazakhstan	5,498
Uzbekistan	Tajikistan	6,468

TCI = trade complementarity index, TII = trade intensity index.
Source: World Bank. World International Trade Solution.
https://wits.worldbank.org/ (accessed 8 June 2020).

Balassa's Revealed Comparative Advantage Index (RCAI) https://wits.worldbank.org/wits/wits/witshelp/Content/Utilities/e1.trade_indicators.htm. RCAI is measured by the product k's share in the country i's exports in relation to its share in the world trade, thus:

$$RCAI_{ik} = x_{ik}/x_{wk},$$

where x_{ij} is the share of product k in total exports of country and i, x_{wk} is the share of product in total world exports. The value of index of more than 1 indicates that the country has a revealed comparative advantage in the product.

Table A3: Selected Revealed Comparative Advantage Index Values for Kazakhstan and Uzbekistan, 2018

HS Code	Product	RCAI
Kazakhstan, Products with Top 10 RCAI Values		
2819	Chromium oxides and hydroxides	106.2
2844	Radioactive chemical elements and radioactive isotopes	61.0
2524	Asbestos	58.9
1204	Linseed, whether or not broken	53.4
2503	Sulfur of all kinds	46.1
1101	Wheat or meslin flour	28.9
7405	Master alloys of copper	25.2
7202	Ferroalloys	23.6
2610	Chromium ores and concentrates	17.2
2709	Petroleum oils and oils obtained from bituminous minerals; crude	16.0

continued on next page

Table A3 *continued*

HS Code	Product	RCAI
\multicolumn{3}{c}{**Uzbekistan, Products with Top 10 RCAI Values**}		
5003	Silk waste	332.8
5002	Raw silk (not thrown)	115.6
5205	Cotton yarn (other than sewing thread)	111.3
0809	Apricots, cherries, peaches (including nectarines)	64.9
5202	Cotton waste	60.5
8102	Molybdenum and articles thereof	51.0
4706	Pulps of fibers derived from recovered paper or paperboard or of other fibrous cellulosic material	45.8
5802	Terry toweling and similar woven terry fabrics	43.3
0806	Grapes, fresh or dried	29.8
0713	Vegetables, leguminous; shelled, whether or not skinned or split, dried	27.9

HS = Harmonized System, RCAI = revealed comparative advantage index.
Source: World Bank. *World International Trade Solution.* https://wits.worldbank.org/ (accessed 8 June 2020).

Forecasting Intra-corridor Trade

The projections for trade within STKEC are developed in two stages: (i) forecasting of trade values among Kazakhstan, Tajikistan, and Uzbekistan; and (ii) forecasting of STKEC parts' shares in this inter-country trade.

The key assumption for all these forecasts is that while current trade values are low (compared to the potential for trade the countries have), these trade flows were growing very fast for 2010-2018. So, the recent growth rates are applied to the change in trade flows between 2018 and 2025 and 2030. The forecast should also consider the general economic growth that is to happen in the next 10 years, so instead of making projections for nominal trade flow values, these flows' gross domestic product (GDP) shares are forecasted. Another assumption is that the shares of STKEC parts (i.e., Shymkent and Turkestan oblasts for Kazakhstan, Sugd oblast for Tajikistan, and Tashkent city and Tashkent oblast for Uzbekistan) in their respective bilateral trade flows are going to increase to some extent. Thus, it is assumed that these areas are going to be the main beneficiaries of the economic corridor development, so the trade among them will grow faster than the trade between countries. However, there are limits to the growth of these city and/or oblast shares in a bilateral trade as other parts of these three countries are also expected to expand their mutual trades.

Thus, the forecasting process implies the following steps:

- calculating these countries' GDP values till 2030;
- calculating the growth of the exports and/or GDP ratio for each pair of countries for 2025 and 2030;
- calculating exports for each pair of countries for 2025 and 2030;
- calculating the shares of exports from one part of STKEC to another in their exporting country's exports for 2025 and 2030; and
- calculating the trade flows between different parts of the STKEC.

To formalize these assumptions, the following notations are used:

$i, j = \{S, T, K\}$ – part of STKEC (S – Shymkent and Turkestan oblast, T – Tashkent city and oblast,

K – Khujand and Sugd oblast),

$m, n = \{KZ, TJ, UZ\}$ – country of the region,

$t = \{2018, 2025, 2030\}$ – year,

$X_t^{m,n}$ or $X_t^{i,j}$ – exports from country m to country n or from part i to part j in year t,

Y_t^{m} – GDP of country m in year t,

gy_m – annual GDP growth rate for country m,

gx_m^n – annual growth rate of $X_t^{m,n}/Y_t^{m}$,

$sx_t^{i,j}$ – share of $X_t^{i,j}$ in $X_t^{m,n}$ (i, m and j, n refer to the same country, e.g., this is a share of exports from Sugd oblast to Tashkent city and Tashkent oblast in total exports from Tajikistan to Uzbekistan) in year t.

Using these notations, the forecasting algorithm consists of the following sequence of formula:

$$Y_t^{m} = Y_{2018}^{m} (1 + gy_m)^{t-2018}, t = \{2025, 2030\}$$

$$X_t^{m,n} = \left(\frac{X_{2018}^{m,n}}{Y_{2018}^{m}} + gx_m^n (t - 2018) \right) Y_t^{m}, t = \{2025, 2030\},$$

$$X_t^{i,j} = sx_t^{i,j} X_t^{m,n}.$$

It is assumed that annual GDP growth rates during 2018–2030 will be 4% for Kazakhstan and 5% for Tajikistan and Uzbekistan. The values of gx_m^n were estimated based on actual data on trade among the countries during 2010–2018.

For $sx_t^{i,j}$, the following assumption was used: if this share is very small (<5%), it is expected to double in the next period of time (e.g., between 2018 and 2025); if it is moderate (<20%), then it is expected to grow 1.5 times in the next period; and if it is significant (≥20%), it is expected to stay unchanged.

References

Asian Development Bank (ADB). 2006. *Central Asia: Increasing Gains from Trade through Regional Cooperation in Trade Policy, Transport, and Customs Transit*. Manila.

_____. 2020a. *CAREC Corridor Performance Measurement and Monitoring: Annual Report 2019*. Manila.

_____. 2020b. *CAREC Transport Strategy 2030*. Manila.

Agency on Statistics under the President of the Republic of Tajikistan. https://www.stat.tj/en (accessed on 8 June 2020).

CAREC Secretariat. 2019. *CAREC CPMM Annual Report*. Manila.

Central Bank of the Republic of Uzbekistan. https://cbu.uz/en/ (accessed on 8 June 2020).

Customs Service, Government of the Republic of Tajikistan. https://tamognia.tj/ (accessed on 8 June 2020).

ESCAP and World Bank: International Trade Costs Database. https://databank.worldbank.org/source/escap-world-bank:-international-trade-costs# (accessed on 8 June 2020).

Kaminski, B. and S. Mitra. 2012. *Borderless Bazaars and Regional Integration in Central Asia: Emerging Patterns of Trade and Cross-Border Cooperation*. Washington, DC: World Bank Group.

Khaknazar, U. 2014. The Accession of Uzbekistan to the CIS Free Trade Agreement: The Union without Commitments? *Bridges*. 7(2). pp. 24-27. (in Russian language).

National Bank of the Republic of Kazakhstan. https://www.nationalbank.kz/?&switch=english (accessed on 8 June 2020).

The Observatory of Economic Complexity. *Product Space*. https://oec.world/en/ (accessed on 8 June 2020).

United Nations Statistics Division. *United Nations Commodity Trade Statistics Database* (UN Comtrade). https://comtrade.un.org/db/default.aspx (accessed on 8 June 2020).

World Bank Group. 2019. *Doing Business 2020*. Washington, DC.

World Bank. *World Integrated Trade Solution*. https://wits.worldbank.org/wits/wits/witshelp/Content/Utilities/e1.trade_indicators.htm (accessed on 8 June 2020).